SACRED SMOKE AND MOUNTAIN SPIRITS

The Art of Appalachian Incense and Smudging

Ivy Mae

Welcome and thank you for picking up our book! If you find enjoyment and value in these pages, please consider leaving a review. Your thoughts and support are greatly appreciated and help others discover our work. Happy reading! ☺

Sacred Smoke and Mountain Spirits:
The Art of Appalachian Incense and Smudging by Ivy Mae

Published by Chek Publishing

Printed in United States of America

First Edition

CONTENTS

Chapter 4:
Trees and Resins of Power 61

Chapter 5:
Crafting Your Incense 71

Chapter 6:
The Art of Smudging 89

Introduction

The Role of Smoke in Appalachian Magic and Its Spiritual Significance

In the heart of the Appalachian mountains, where the ancient forests stand as timeless guardians over the rolling hills and hidden valleys, there exists a tradition that threads through the fabric of life like the meandering rivers that sculpt the landscape. This tradition, rooted in the sacred essence of smoke, is more than a mere practice; it is a living, breathing testament to the deep spiritual connection between the land, its people, and the unseen forces that govern the natural world. In this realm, where the veil between the physical and spiritual is as thin as the morning mist, smoke becomes a sacred vessel, a bridge that connects the heart of the earth to the vast expanse of the cosmos. The role of smoke in Appalachian magic, therefore, is not merely functional; it is profoundly spiritual, an integral component of a rich tapestry of beliefs and practices that have been passed down through generations, whispered in the winds, and echoed in the songs of the birds.

Smoke as a Conduit

To understand the role of smoke in Appalachian magic is to delve into the heart of a tradition where every leaf, twig, and stone is imbued with meaning, and every wisp of smoke carries with it the prayers, intentions, and dreams of those who walk this sacred path. In this world, smoke is the breath of the earth, a physical manifestation of the life force that animates all things. It is through smoke that the magicians, healers, and guardians of these ancient traditions communicate with the spirits of the land, the ancestors who walked before, and the myriad entities that inhabit the unseen realms.

The use of smoke in ritual and daily life is multifaceted, serving not only as a means of purification and protection but also as a vehicle for transformation. When herbs, resins, and woods, each carefully chosen for their spiritual and magical properties, are offered to the fire, the resulting smoke becomes a potent tool. It carries the essence of the materials, transformed by the sacred flame, to the spirits, the gods, and the ancestors, serving as an offering, a plea, or a thanksgiving. This smoke, which dances and swirls to the rhythms of the wind, is seen as a living entity, a messenger that transcends the boundaries of the physical world, carrying the hopes and wishes of the practitioner to the ears of the divine.

Spiritual Significance

The spiritual significance of smoke in Appalachian traditions is as layered and complex as the mountains themselves, each ridge and valley holding its own story, its own spirit. Smoke is not merely a byproduct of fire; it is a symbol of the eternal cycle of life, death, and rebirth, a reminder of the impermanence of all things and the eternal flow of the universe. In the act of burning sacred substances, there is a recognition of the transitory nature of the physical form, an acknowledgment that from the ashes, new life will spring forth.

Smoke is also seen as a purifying force, capable of cleansing not only the physical space but also the spiritual and emotional realms. It is believed that as smoke rises, it carries away negativity, stagnant energies, and the shadows that cling to the soul, leaving in its wake a sense of peace, clarity, and renewal. This act of purification is central to many Appalachian rituals, from the simple cleansing of a new home to the more complex ceremonies that mark the significant passages of life.

Furthermore, smoke serves as a protective barrier, a shield against the unseen forces that may seek to disrupt the harmony of the living. By encircling oneself or one's space with the sacred smoke, a boundary is created, a boundary that is respected by the spirits and energies that move within the unseen realms. This protection is not seen as a warding off of evil in the simplistic sense but rather as an affirmation of the sacredness of the space, an assertion of the practitioner's sovereignty over their spiritual and physical domain.

In the whispering of the leaves, the murmuring of the streams, and the gentle crackling of the fire, the deeper spiritual meanings of smoke are revealed. It is a language, a form of communication that transcends words, a dialogue between the heart and the infinite. To work with smoke in this context is to engage in a sacred dance, a dance that honors the interconnectedness of all things, the deep wisdom of the land, and the ancient lineage of those who have practiced this art before.

As we delve deeper into the mysteries of smoke and its role in Appalachian magic, we are invited to step into a world where the boundaries between the seen and unseen blur, where the ancient wisdom of the land whispers in our ears, and where every puff of sacred smoke carries with it a world of meaning, waiting to be explored. This exploration is not merely an academic pursuit but a journey of the soul, a pilgrimage to the very heart of what it means to live in harmony with the natural world and the unseen forces that guide and shape our lives.

Historical and Cultural Roots of Smudging and Incense in Appalachian Traditions

The Appalachian mountains, with their ancient peaks and deep, mystical valleys, have long been a crucible for a diverse tapestry of cultures and traditions. This rich cultural mosaic has given rise to unique practices and beliefs, particularly in the realm of smoke magic, where the art of smudging and incense-making carries the imprint of various peoples who have called these mountains home. Understanding the historical and cultural roots of these practices requires us to delve into the complex interplay of influences that have shaped Appalachian traditions, creating a unique synthesis that is both deeply local and expansively global.

Cultural Syncretism

The practice of using smoke for spiritual, healing, and ritual purposes is a thread that runs through many cultures around the world, and Appalachia is no exception. The region's smoke magic traditions are a vibrant tapestry woven from the threads of Native American, African, European, and even Asian influences, each contributing their own spiritual philosophies, herbal knowledge, and ritual practices to the collective wisdom of the mountains.

Native American tribes, the original inhabitants of these lands, brought with them a profound understanding of the natural world, viewing the act of burning herbs and resins as a way to cleanse spaces, heal the sick, and communicate with the spirit world. Their practices, deeply rooted in a holistic view of the universe where every element is interconnected, laid the foundational stone for what would become Appalachian smoke magic.

The arrival of European settlers, with their own rich traditions of herb lore and folk magic, introduced new elements into the existing practices. These settlers, hailing from a myriad of cultural backgrounds, brought with them the ancient practices of their homelands, from the

Celtic use of smoke in seasonal rituals to the protective incense burnings found in Slavic and Germanic traditions.

The African influence, brought to the Appalachian region through the tragic channels of slavery, added another layer of depth to the region's smoke magic. Enslaved Africans, striving to maintain a connection to their spiritual roots, blended their traditional practices with those they encountered in their new environment, introducing techniques and botanical knowledge that would deeply enrich the Appalachian tradition.

This cultural syncretism, the blending of diverse practices and beliefs, gave rise to a form of smoke magic that is uniquely Appalachian, a tradition that is both a testament to the region's complex history and a living, evolving practice that continues to absorb and adapt influences from new cultures and ideas.

Historical Practices

The integration of smudging and incense-making into the fabric of Appalachian life is a story that mirrors the broader narrative of survival, adaptation, and resistance that characterizes the region's history. These practices, far from being static or monolithic, have evolved over time, shaped by the necessities of life in the mountains and the changing tides of cultural exchange.

In the early days, smudging and incense-making were integral to daily life, serving a multitude of purposes from the mundane to the sacred. The burning of sage, cedar, and sweetgrass for purification was a common practice in homes, a ritual for cleansing the space of negative energies and inviting protection and peace. This practice, deeply rooted in Native American traditions, was quickly adopted and adapted by settlers, merging with European traditions of using smoke for protection during childbirth, to bless crops, and to guard against illness.

Seasonal rituals, marking the turning of the wheel of the year, were also occasions for the use of sacred smoke. These rituals, often blending Native American, European, and later African traditions, used specific herbs and resins chosen for their symbolic significance to the season. The lighting of bonfires during the summer solstice, accompanied by the burning of aromatic herbs, is one such practice that illustrates the syncretism of Appalachian smoke magic, where the Celtic tradition of Midsummer bonfires meets the Native American practice of offering smoke to the spirits.

The use of smoke in healing rituals is another facet of the historical practices of the region. Traditional healers, known in some Appalachian communities as "granny women" or "root doctors," employed smoke as a tool for both physical and spiritual healing. The burning of specific herbs was believed to facilitate the healing process, drawing out illness and imbuing the patient with the strength and protection of the plant spirits. These practices, drawing on a blend of Native American, African, and European herbal knowledge, illustrate the deeply integrative nature of Appalachian smoke magic.

In times of transition and crisis, such as during childbirth, death, or periods of significant change, smudging and incense-making took on a particularly poignant significance. The smoke, with its ability to bridge the worlds, was a comforting and protective presence, a way to ensure safe passage for the soul in times of transition.

The occasions for the use of smoke in Appalachian history are as varied as the people who have practiced this art. From the simple act of cleansing a new home to the complex rituals that mark the high points of the communal calendar, smoke has been a constant companion, a source of strength, protection, and connection to the spiritual realm.

As we reflect on the historical and cultural roots of smudging and incense-making in Appalachian traditions, we are reminded of the resilience of these practices, their ability to adapt and thrive in the face of change. This resilience, this capacity for synthesis and renewal, is at the heart of Appalachian smoke magic, a tradition that continues to evolve, embracing new influences while remaining deeply rooted in the ancient wisdom of the land.

THE INTENTION BEHIND THE BOOK AND GUIDING PRINCIPLES FOR ETHICAL PRACTICE

As we delve deeper into the heart of Appalachian smoke magic, it becomes imperative to articulate the purpose and intentions that have guided the creation of this tome. "Sacred Smoke and Mountain Spirits: The Art of Appalachian Incense and Smudging" is more than a mere collection of practices and recipes; it is a reverent ode to the rich heritage of a land shaped by the whispers of the forests and the spirits of the mountains. Our intention is to bridge the past with the present, to weave the ancient threads of Appalachian lore into the fabric of contemporary spiritual practice, ensuring that the wisdom of the ages is preserved, respected, and honored.

Book's Purpose

The primary purpose of this book is to preserve the rich tapestry of Appalachian smoke magic, a tradition that encompasses not only the practical aspects of smudging and incense making but also the profound spiritual connections these practices foster with the natural world. It is an invitation to explore the deep, mystical roots of Appalachian spirituality, to understand the sacredness imbued in the simple act of lighting herbs and watching the smoke rise, carrying prayers and intentions to the spirits.

Moreover, this work aims to educate readers on the respectful and informed practice of smoke magic, illuminating the ethical considerations that must guide our interactions with the natural world. It is a call to approach these ancient practices with a heart full of reverence, acknowledging the cultural and spiritual legacies that they carry. Through this book, readers are encouraged to foster a deeper connection with the land, to listen to the stories it tells, and to find their own place within the grand, unfolding narrative of Appalachian magic.

Ethical Considerations

At the core of Appalachian smoke magic are principles of respect, sustainability, and harmony with nature. As we venture into the forests and fields in search of herbs, resins, and woods, it is crucial to do so with a mindful awareness of the impact of our actions. Sustainable foraging practices are emphasized, urging practitioners to take only what is needed, to harvest in a way that ensures the continued health and vitality of plant populations, and to always offer gratitude to the land for its gifts.

Acknowledging the origins of specific practices is another fundamental aspect of ethical engagement with smoke magic. This involves recognizing the diverse cultural influences that have shaped Appalachian traditions and honoring the contributions of Native American, African, European, and other peoples to this rich spiritual heritage. Practitioners are encouraged to approach these traditions with humility and openness, seeking to understand their historical and cultural contexts.

Respecting the land and its spirits is perhaps the most sacred duty of the smoke magic practitioner. This means recognizing the land as a living, sentient being, replete with its own wisdom, spirits, and energies. Engaging with the land in a way that honors its sanctity, listening to its

needs, and protecting its integrity is essential for maintaining the balance and harmony that are the foundation of Appalachian spirituality.

Invitation to the Reader

This book extends a heartfelt invitation to all who feel the call of the mountains, the allure of the ancient forests, and the pull of the sacred smoke. Whether you are a seasoned practitioner of smoke magic or a curious seeker new to these paths, you are welcomed into a journey of discovery, learning, and deep spiritual connection. It is an invitation to open your heart and mind, to explore the rich tapestry of Appalachian smoke magic with reverence and respect, and to integrate these ancient practices into your life in a way that honors the traditions, the land, and the spirits.

As you turn these pages, allow yourself to be transported to the mist-shrouded hills of Appalachia, to walk in the footsteps of the ancestors, and to breathe in the sacred smoke that has been a bridge between worlds for generations. Embark on this journey with an open heart, ready to learn, to grow, and to deepen your connection with the natural world and the unseen forces that weave through the tapestry of life.

In doing so, you become a guardian of a precious heritage, a keeper of ancient wisdom, and a participant in the sacred dance of smoke and spirit that is the heart of Appalachian magic. Welcome to the path of sacred smoke and mountain spirits, where every breath is a prayer, and every plume of smoke carries the whispers of the ancient ones, inviting you to remember, to reconnect, and to reawaken to the magic that flows through the land, through the smoke, and through your own soul.

Chapter 1:
Foundations of Smoke Magic

UNDERSTANDING THE BASICS OF SMOKE MAGIC AND ITS APPLICATIONS

In the dappled light of the Appalachian forests, where the air carries the scent of pine and the earth holds the whispers of ages, lies a practice as ancient as the mountains themselves. This practice, known as smoke magic, is the art of harnessing the ethereal qualities of smoke to bridge the physical and spiritual worlds, to cleanse, protect, and communicate with forces seen and unseen. It is here, amidst the rolling hills and verdant valleys of Appalachia, that smoke magic finds a unique expression, woven into the fabric of daily life and imbued with the rich tapestry of folklore that colors the region.

Introduction to Smoke Magic

Smoke magic, at its core, is the use of smoke as a conduit for intention, prayer, and transformation. This practice transcends cultural boundaries, finding a place in nearly every spiritual tradition around the world. In the Appalachian context, smoke magic draws from the land's abundant natural resources and the diverse cultural heritage of its people, creating a practice that is both deeply local and universally resonant.

At the heart of smoke magic is the understanding that smoke acts as a vehicle for the spirit, capable of carrying messages to the divine, purifying the physical and etheric bodies, and altering the energetic composition of a space or object. The act of burning sacred herbs, resins, and woods, and the resulting smoke, is laden with symbolic meaning, each element chosen for its specific properties and the intentions of the practitioner.

Applications of Smoke Magic

The applications of smoke magic are as varied as the practitioners who wield it, each finding unique ways to integrate this practice into their spiritual and daily lives. Here, in the Appalachian tradition, smoke magic serves multiple purposes, deeply rooted in the needs and rhythms of mountain life.

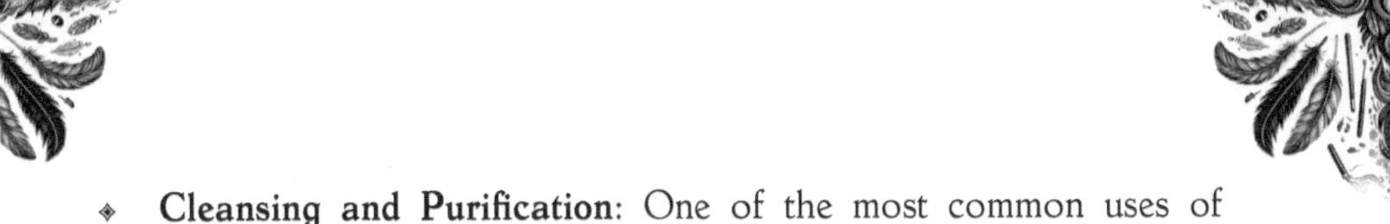

- **Cleansing and Purification**: One of the most common uses of smoke magic is for the cleansing and purification of spaces, objects, and individuals. In Appalachia, this often involves the burning of native herbs like sage, cedar, and sweetgrass. The smoke from these plants is believed to clear away negative energies and spirits, making room for positive influences and protection. A classic example is the smudging of a new home to cleanse it of past energies and to bless it for the future.

- **Communication with the Spirit Realm**: Smoke is also used as a medium for communication with the spirit world. It is believed that as smoke rises, it carries prayers and intentions from the physical realm to the spiritual, making it an essential element in rituals and ceremonies. Appalachian lore is rich with tales of smoke being used to commune with ancestors, nature spirits, and deities, facilitating a dialogue between worlds.

- **Enhancement of Meditation and Divination**: The use of smoke in meditation and divination practices is another cornerstone of smoke magic. The scent and sight of smoke can induce a trance-like state, opening the practitioner to deeper insights and spiritual experiences. Incense made from local herbs and resins is often used in these practices, chosen for its ability to elevate the mind and enhance psychic abilities.

- **Carrying Prayers and Intentions**: In Appalachian smoke magic, the act of burning herbs and watching the smoke rise is a physical representation of sending prayers and intentions into the universe. This practice is often used in spellwork and rituals, where the smoke's direction and behavior are observed as omens or messages from the spirit realm.

The Symbolic Meanings of Smoke in Appalachian Folklore

In Appalachian folklore, smoke carries with it a wealth of symbolic meanings, each rooted in the observation of nature and the intuitive understanding of the world's hidden currents. Smoke is often seen as a symbol of transformation and transcendence, representing the soul's journey from the physical plane to the spiritual. It is also associated with the element of air, embodying qualities of communication, intellect, and the unseen forces that shape our lives.

The direction and movement of smoke are also imbued with meaning. For instance, smoke that rises straight and true is seen as a sign of fa-

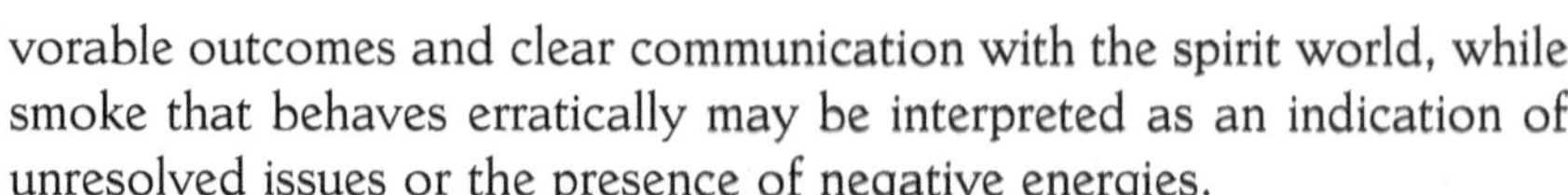

vorable outcomes and clear communication with the spirit world, while smoke that behaves erratically may be interpreted as an indication of unresolved issues or the presence of negative energies.

Moreover, the choice of material to be burned is deeply symbolic, with each herb, resin, and wood carrying its own set of associations and energies. For example, sage is often associated with wisdom and purification, cedar with protection and healing, and sweetgrass with blessing and attracting positive spirits.

In this chapter, we delve into these foundational aspects of smoke magic, exploring the rich tapestry of practices, symbols, and meanings that make up this ancient art. Through the lens of Appalachian traditions, we will uncover the universal threads that connect smoke magic to the broader tapestry of spiritual practice, offering insights and inspiration for practitioners both within and beyond the Appalachian region.

THE SYMBOLIC MEANINGS OF SMOKE IN APPALACHIAN FOLKLORE

In the tapestry of Appalachian folklore, smoke weaves a narrative rich with symbolism and mystery, serving as a poignant reminder of life's transient nature and the ever-present connection between the corporeal and the ethereal realms. The art of smoke magic, deeply embedded in the cultural fabric of Appalachia, is a testament to the profound understanding of smoke's power and its place in the natural and spiritual worlds. This section delves into the multifaceted symbolism of smoke and its manifestations in the folklore and daily practices of the Appalachian people, offering a glimpse into the soul of a tradition where the veil between worlds is as thin as a wisp of smoke.

Smoke as a Symbol

Transformation and Transcendence

In Appalachian lore, smoke is emblematic of transformation, a visual representation of the metamorphosis from solid to ethereal, from material to spiritual. This symbolism is rooted in the act of burning — a process of change wherein the physical form of herbs, resins, and woods is transmuted into smoke, ascending towards the heavens. This transformation is a mirror to life's impermanence, a reminder that all things must pass through the crucible of change. In rituals and ceremonies, the use of smoke encapsulates this philosophy, with each billow carrying away the old, making way for the new.

The Ephemeral Nature of Life

Smoke's fleeting nature, its tendency to dissipate into the air, speaks to the ephemeral quality of life itself. Appalachian tales and practices often reflect this understanding, imbuing smoke with a sense of sacredness and respect for the transient moments of existence. The use of smoke in marking life's significant passages — births, deaths, and the turning of the year's wheel — serves as a poignant acknowledgment of life's fleeting beauty and the importance of cherishing each moment.

Bridge Between Worlds

Perhaps the most profound symbolism attributed to smoke in Appalachian folklore is its role as a bridge between the physical and spiritual worlds. Smoke's ascent from earth to sky is seen as a path for prayers and intentions to reach the divine, and for messages from the spirit realm to be delivered to the mortal plane. This concept is integral to smoke magic practices, where smoke is not just a tool but a sacred medium of communication, connecting the hearts and minds of practitioners with the vast unseen.

Folklore and Smoke

Appalachian folklore is rife with tales that highlight the significance of smoke in spiritual and protective practices. These stories, passed down through generations, are not mere entertainment but carry the weight of ancestral wisdom and cultural identity.

Tales of Protection and Warding

One common motif in Appalachian folklore involves characters using smoke for protection against malevolent forces. Tales of wise women and cunning folk creating smudge sticks from protective herbs like sage and cedar to ward off evil spirits are a testament to smoke's protective power. These narratives often depict smoke as an impenetrable barrier, a shield that guards the home and its inhabitants from unseen dangers.

Divination and Communication

Another recurring theme is the use of smoke in divination and communication with otherworldly entities. Stories tell of seers gazing into the swirling patterns of incense smoke to divine the future or receive guidance from ancestors and spirits. These tales underscore the belief in smoke's ability to open portals to other realms, offering a glimpse into the mysteries beyond our mortal understanding.

Folklore as Cultural Memory

The folklore surrounding smoke magic in Appalachia serves as a cultural memory, a repository of collective wisdom and tradition. Each story, with its depiction of smoke's power and significance, contributes to the cultural understanding and reverence for smoke magic in the region. These narratives not only entertain but educate, instilling in listeners a deep respect for the natural world and the unseen forces that permeate it.

Through the exploration of smoke's symbolism and its presence in Appalachian folklore, we gain insight into the spiritual landscape of the region, where the natural and the supernatural coalesce. Smoke, in its ethereal grace, embodies the profound connections that bind the physical to the spiritual, serving as a constant reminder of the world's magic that surrounds and permeates us. In the wisps of smoke that rise from the smoldering embers of an Appalachian hearth, we find the essence of a tradition that honors the sacred dance of life, death, and rebirth, inviting us to look beyond the veil and embrace the mysteries that lie beyond.

Concluding Thoughts

As we draw the curtain on the first chapter of our journey into the heart of Appalachian smoke magic, we find ourselves standing at the threshold of a world where the ancient whispers of the earth and the gentle sighs of the spirit realm converge in the delicate dance of smoke. "Foundations of Smoke Magic" has served as our gateway into understanding the profound depths and the ethereal heights of this venerable practice, illuminating the path with the flickering light of tradition and folklore.

We have traversed the landscape of smoke magic, exploring its multifaceted applications — from the cleansing of spaces and spirits to the sacred act of communication with the divine. Each plume of smoke, rising and twisting into the infinite, carries with it the intentions, prayers, and voices of generations past and present, weaving a tapestry of connection that transcends the bounds of time and space.

The stories and symbols that permeate Appalachian folklore have lent us their wisdom, revealing smoke as a symbol of life's ephemeral nature, a reminder of the constant flow of transformation that governs all existence. These tales, rich with the hues of human experience and the colors of the natural world, have painted a picture of smoke as a guardian, a guide, and a bridge between worlds, imbuing our understanding with a reverence for the sacred dance of life and death.

As we move forward in our exploration of "Sacred Smoke and Mountain Spirits," let us carry with us the lessons gleaned from this foundational chapter. Let the knowledge of smoke's power and purpose guide our steps as we delve deeper into the art of Appalachian incense and smudging, armed with a newfound respect for the traditions that have been entrusted to us by the land and its stewards.

May the smoke that rises from our altars, hearths, and hearts be a testament to the enduring bond between humanity and the natural world, a fragrant offering to the spirits that walk beside us, and a beacon of light illuminating our path towards deeper understanding and spiritual fulfillment.

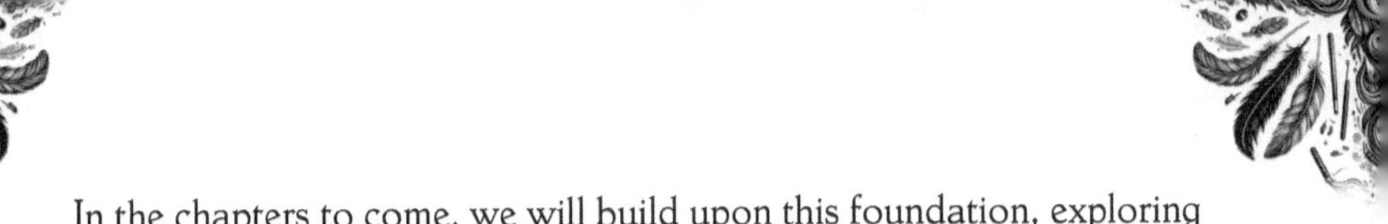

In the chapters to come, we will build upon this foundation, exploring the rich tapestry of plants and practices that make up the Appalachian tradition of smoke magic. Together, we will discover the ways in which these ancient practices can be woven into the fabric of our modern lives, bringing healing, protection, and a deeper connection to the spirits of the land.

So, let us step forward with open hearts and curious minds, ready to embrace the mysteries and marvels that await us in the smoke-scented pages of this book. The journey has only just begun, and the spirits of the mountains, rivers, and forests are calling us home, to a place where the sacred smoke rises, and the mountain spirits dance in the dappled light of a world reborn through magic.

Chapter 2:
Ethical Foraging and Harvesting

GUIDELINES FOR ETHICAL AND SUSTAINABLE FORAGING OF HERBS, RESINS, AND WOODS IN THE APPALACHIAN REGION

In the verdant expanse of the Appalachian region, where the land whispers ancient secrets and the breeze carries the scent of myriad herbs, trees, and resins, lies a sacred tradition of foraging that is as old as the mountains themselves. Chapter 2, "Ethical Foraging and Harvesting," serves as a guide to navigating this hallowed practice with reverence, respect, and a deep sense of stewardship towards the Earth and its plentiful bounty. Herein, we explore the nuanced principles of ethical foraging, ensuring that our actions contribute to the preservation and flourishing of the land that offers us its gifts.

Principles of Ethical Foraging

The act of foraging, while a physical endeavor, begins with a mindset—a mindset that acknowledges our place within the larger web of life and our responsibility towards it. Ethical foraging transcends mere gathering; it is an act of communion with nature, a dialogue between forager and flora that respects the sacred balance of life.

Respect for the Land

The first tenet of ethical foraging is a profound respect for the land. This respect dictates that we approach foraging with mindfulness, recognizing that we are guests in a landscape teeming with life, each plant and tree a vital thread in the tapestry of the ecosystem. It requires us to forage in a way that leaves minimal impact, ensuring that our footsteps are light and our presence benign.

Sustainability: Taking Only What Is Needed

Central to the practice of ethical foraging is the principle of sustainability. This means taking only what we need, never more, and always ensuring that what we take does not harm the plant's ability to thrive and reproduce. It's about understanding the life cycle of the plants we forage, knowing the right time to harvest so that the plant can regen-

erate, and ensuring that enough remains for wildlife and for the plant's continued presence in the ecosystem.

Ecological Role and Habitat Consideration

Each plant plays a unique role in its habitat, contributing to the ecological balance and providing food and shelter for wildlife. Ethical foraging requires an understanding of these roles and a careful consideration of how removing a plant or part of it might impact the surrounding environment. It involves learning about the plants that are abundant and those that are rare or sensitive, and making foraging choices that prioritize the health and diversity of the ecosystem.

Foraging Permissions

Foraging is not just about what we take but also where we take it from. The landscapes of Appalachia are a patchwork of private lands, public forests, and protected areas, each with its own set of rules and expectations.

Legal and Ethical Considerations

Before foraging, it is crucial to be aware of the legal considerations that govern the land. This includes understanding which areas are open to public foraging, which plants are protected under law, and the regulations specific to national parks, state forests, and other protected areas. Ethical foraging respects these regulations, recognizing them as measures put in place to protect and preserve the natural heritage of the region.

Respecting Land Ownership and Community Values

Foraging on private land without permission is not only illegal but also a violation of the principles of ethical foraging. It is essential to seek the landowner's consent, engaging with them in a manner that is respectful and transparent. Many landowners are stewards of the land in their own right, and forging respectful relationships with them can lead to mutually beneficial arrangements that honor the land and its resources.

Supporting the Local Ecosystem

Ethical foraging is inherently local, focused on building a sustainable relationship with the immediate environment. It involves choosing native plants over invasive species, fostering biodiversity, and contributing to the health of the local ecosystem. By foraging responsibly, we support the intricate balance of life that defines the Appalachian land-

scape, ensuring that its beauty and abundance remain for generations to come.

In this chapter, we delve into the heart of ethical foraging, guided by principles that honor the land and its spirits. It is a journey of learning to listen to the whispers of the Earth, to understand the language of the plants and trees, and to gather with a heart full of gratitude and hands that seek to heal and preserve. As we walk the paths of the Appalachian forests, may we do so with a deep awareness of the sacredness of our actions, forging a bond with the land that is rooted in respect, stewardship, and an enduring commitment to the well-being of the natural world.

RECOGNIZING AND RESPECTING THE SPIRITS OF THE LAND

In the verdant heart of Appalachia, where each leaf and stone pulses with ancient wisdom, the act of foraging transcends mere collection; it becomes a sacred dialogue between the forager and the myriad spirits that guard and enliven the land. Recognizing and respecting these spirits is not just a matter of tradition but a profound acknowledgment of the deep interconnectedness that binds all life. This section explores the spiritual underpinnings of foraging in the Appalachian wilderness, guiding practitioners in engaging with the land in a manner that honors the unseen forces that watch over it.

Spiritual Connection

The Appalachian tradition is steeped in a rich understanding of the land as a living, breathing entity, imbued with spirits that oversee the natural order. These spirits, revered as guardians of the forests, rivers, and mountains, are integral to the ecological balance and are believed to imbue the land's flora and fauna with life force and vitality. To forage within these sacred bounds is to step into a realm of deep spiritual significance, where each plant is seen not merely as a resource but as a living being, ensouled and sacred.

Approaching foraging with this reverence involves more than an acknowledgment of the physical ecosystem; it requires a recognition of the spiritual essence that permeates the landscape. Practitioners are encouraged to attune their senses to the subtle energies of the land, to listen for the whispers of the spirits, and to approach each foraging endeavor with a heart open to receiving the wisdom and blessings these entities bestow.

Acknowledging the Spirits

Before embarking on a foraging journey, it is customary to pause and acknowledge the presence of the land's spirits, offering a silent or spoken greeting and expressing the intention to forage with respect and gratitude. This acknowledgment is a gesture of humility and recogni-

tion of the spirits' dominion over the land, setting the tone for a foraging practice that is in harmony with the spiritual ecosystem.

Offering Gratitude

Gratitude is the cornerstone of a respectful foraging practice. It is an expression of appreciation for the bounty the land provides and an acknowledgment of the interconnectedness of all life. Offering thanks can be as simple as a whispered word of gratitude, a heartfelt thought directed towards the spirits, or a moment of silent reflection on the abundance and generosity of nature.

Rituals and Offerings

The act of making offerings or performing rituals before or after foraging is a tangible expression of reverence for the spirits of the land and the plants themselves. These practices serve to strengthen the bond between the forager and the natural world, creating a reciprocal relationship rooted in respect and mutual benefit.

Simple Offerings

Offerings are a way to give back to the land, to compensate for what has been taken, and to honor the spirit of the plant or the guardians of the place. Traditional offerings might include a strand of hair, symbolizing a personal connection and the offering of a part of oneself; a small stone or crystal, as a gift of the earth back to itself; or a libation of water, symbolizing life and vitality. The nature of the offering is less important than the intention behind it, which should be one of heartfelt gratitude and respect.

Rituals of Thanks and Cleansing

Engaging in a ritual of thanks is a powerful way to conclude a foraging expedition, serving as a closing of the sacred space and an acknowledgment of the gifts received. This might involve a moment of quiet reflection, a prayer, or a simple ceremony wherein the forager shares a piece of the harvest with the land, leaving it as an offering to the spirits.

Cleansing rituals post-foraging are also significant, serving to restore balance and ensure that no unwanted energies are carried back from the wilderness. This might involve the use of smoke from sacred herbs, a ritual washing of hands and feet in a natural body of water, or the use of sound, such as bells or chimes, to dispel any lingering energies.

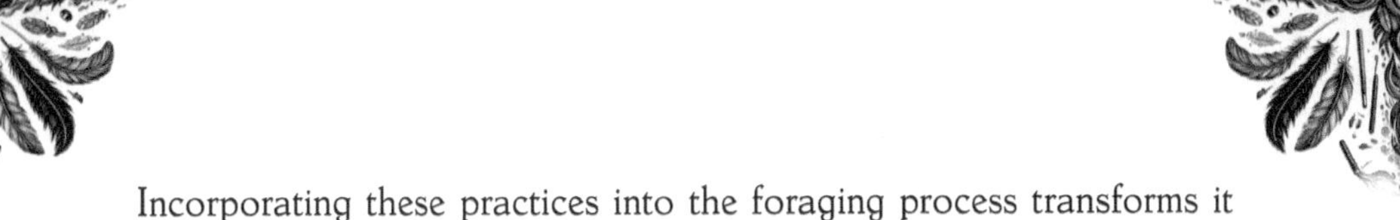

Incorporating these practices into the foraging process transforms it from a mere act of gathering into a deeply spiritual experience, one that honors the ancient pact between humans and the natural world. By recognizing and respecting the spirits of the land, foragers step into a role that is as old as the mountains themselves — that of the steward, the guardian, and the humble supplicant, walking in harmony with the unseen forces that animate the world. In this way, the tradition of ethical foraging in Appalachia becomes a sacred dance with the land, a mutual exchange of blessings and respect that nourishes both the body and the soul.

Appalachian Foraging Thanks and Cleansing Ritual

As the sun dips below the horizon, painting the Appalachian sky with strokes of crimson and gold, a time-honored ritual unfolds, marking the conclusion of a day's foraging and the restoration of balance between forager and the natural world. This Thanks and Cleansing Ritual, steeped in the traditions of the mountains, serves as a profound gesture of gratitude to the spirits of the land and a purification of the forager's energy, ensuring harmony remains within and around.

Materials Needed:

◈ A small bundle of locally foraged herbs, such as sage, lavender, or cedar, tied with a natural twine, symbolizing the gifts of the land.

◈ A clear, natural water source, such as a stream, river, or collected rainwater, for the cleansing part of the ritual.

◈ A smooth, flat stone, found during the foraging journey, to serve as an altar or offering platform.

Preparation: Choose a quiet spot in nature, preferably where the foraging took place, where the sounds of civilization fade and the whispers of the earth can be heard. This sacred space, surrounded by the bounty of the land, becomes the setting for the ritual, a bridge between the heart of the forager and the spirit of Appalachia.

Location: An undisturbed area within the foraging site, where the earth's energy is palpable, and the presence of the land's spirits can be felt. This could be a clearing in the woods, beside a babbling brook, or within a meadow teeming with wildflowers.

Timing: The ritual is most potent at dusk, as the day gives way to night, symbolizing the transition from activity to rest, from giving to receiving.

Procedure:

1. **Herb Bundle Consecration:** Begin by holding the herb bundle gently in your hands. Close your eyes and take a deep breath, grounding yourself in the present moment. Consecrate the bundle with a whisper, "Gifts of the earth, bearers of the land's essence, I offer you back to the soil as a token of my deepest gratitude."

2. **Stone Altar Preparation:** Place the smooth stone on the ground before you, envisioning it as an altar to the spirits of the land. Gently lay the herb bundle atop the stone, arranging it with care and reverence.

3. **Gratitude Offering:** Stand or kneel before the stone altar, and in the quiet of the twilight, offer your thanks. Speak from the heart, expressing gratitude for the abundance shared by the land, for the guidance of the spirits, and for the sacred connection fostered through foraging.

4. **Cleansing Ritual:** Approach the water source with respect, acknowledging its purity and life-giving essence. Using your hands or a small vessel, scoop up some water. Gently sprinkle the water over the herb bundle, over the stone, and lastly over your hands, symbolizing the cleansing of the harvest, the land, and yourself. As you do so, envision any residual energies being washed away, restoring balance and peace.

5. **Closing Blessing:** With the cleansing complete, offer a final blessing to close the ritual. You might say, "With water and herb, I honor the cycle of give and take, of harvest and return. May the balance be preserved, and the bond between forager and earth be strengthened. Blessed be."

6. **Ritual Conclusion:** As night fully embraces the land, take a moment to feel the energy of the ritual space. When ready, gently leave the herb bundle on the stone altar as an offering to the spirits and slowly retreat from the space, carrying with you the peace and purity instilled by the ritual.

Aftercare: Carry the sense of gratitude and balance with you as you leave the foraging site, allowing the experience of the ritual to infuse your daily life with a deeper appreciation for the natural world.

Notes/Warnings: Ensure the chosen ritual site is safe and will not be disturbed. Practice caution near water sources, and be mindful of the natural environment, leaving no trace of your presence.

Variations: To personalize the ritual, consider incorporating elements significant to your personal practice or reflective of the specific area in which you forage. This might include singing a traditional Appalachian folk song, reciting a poem inspired by the landscape, or simply sitting in silent meditation to fully absorb the spirit of the land.

Through this Thanks and Cleansing Ritual, the forager not only honors the age-old traditions of Appalachia but also reaffirms a commitment to walking gently upon the earth, ensuring that the sacred dance of giving and receiving continues in harmony for generations to come.

SEASONAL FORAGING CALENDAR AND BEST PRACTICES

In the heart of Appalachia, where the mountains breathe with the seasons and the land sings the song of time, foraging is not just an act of gathering but a rhythmic dance with nature. The Seasonal Foraging Calendar and Best Practices serve as a compass, guiding practitioners through the ebb and flow of the year, ensuring that each step and each harvest is in harmony with the natural cycle. This section delves into the wisdom of seasonal rhythms and the art of foraging with respect, care, and a deep understanding of the land's offerings.

Seasonal Rhythms: The Appalachian Foraging Calendar

The Appalachian region, with its diverse ecosystems and rich biodiversity, presents a unique foraging calendar, marked by the changing seasons and the specific offerings each brings. This calendar is not just a schedule of availability but a testament to the deep connection between the land and its inhabitants, a guide for syncing human activity with the natural world.

Spring: Awakening and Renewal

As the snow melts and the first green shoots emerge, spring beckons foragers to the awakening woods. This is the time for tender greens and early blooms, each carrying the fresh energy of renewal.

- **March to April**: Look for ramps (wild leeks), morels, and the bright yellow blooms of forsythia, which signal the revival of the land. Nettle, with its deep green leaves, offers a potent spring tonic, rich in minerals and vitality.

- **Late April to May**: This period sees the emergence of dandelion greens, violets, and the first of the wild strawberries. Birch and maple trees begin to offer their sap, a sweet elixir of the season.

Summer: Abundance and Vitality

Summer in Appalachia is a time of lush abundance, with the land overflowing with herbs, berries, and flowers. The long days and warm nights bring forth a bounty that is both diverse and plentiful.

- **June to July**: Wild roses, chamomile, and lavender grace the landscape with their aromatic presence. Blackberries, blueberries, and raspberries offer their juicy sweetness, while the forests hide chanterelle mushrooms and the fragrant linden flowers.

- **August**: As summer reaches its zenith, elderberries, goldenrod, and the deep purple of pokeberries make their appearance, alongside the medicinal jewelweed, known for its soothing properties.

Autumn: Harvest and Preparation

Autumn is a time of gathering and preparing, of honoring the year's bounty and ensuring the land's gifts are preserved for the colder months ahead.

- **September to October**: The forests and fields are rich with roots like burdock and yellow dock, while the trees offer hickory nuts and walnuts. This is also the time for wild apples and pears, their crisp sweetness a hallmark of the season.

- **Late October to November**: As the leaves turn, it's time to collect the last of the herbs before the first frost, including sage, thyme, and rosemary. Pine, cedar, and spruce resins begin to harden, perfect for harvesting.

Winter: Reflection and Anticipation

Winter in Appalachia is a quiet time, a period of reflection and anticipation for the cycle to begin anew. While foraging opportunities are fewer, the season still offers gifts for those who know where to look.

- **December to February**: The bark of birch and willow can be collected for their medicinal properties. Evergreens like pine and fir not only offer their needles for teas and infusions but remind us of the enduring life force that pulses beneath the snow.

Foraging Best Practices

Foraging is both an art and a science, requiring knowledge, respect, and a keen awareness of the environment. The following best practices ensure that foraging is done sustainably, safely, and in a way that honors the land and its offerings.

Plant Identification

Correctly identifying plants is foundational to ethical foraging. Misidentification can lead to the harvesting of endangered species or the ingestion of toxic plants. Utilizing our guide in Chapter 3 and Chapter

4, workshops, and the wisdom of experienced foragers to build your knowledge. When in doubt, leave the plant be.

Optimal Times for Harvesting

- ❖ **Time of Day**: The best time to forage is in the morning after the dew has lifted but before the heat of the day. This ensures plants are not wilted and their essential oils are at their peak.

- ❖ **Seasonal Timing**: Pay attention to the life cycle of the plant. Harvest leaves and flowers in the spring and summer when they are most vibrant, roots in the autumn when the plant's energy has returned to the earth, and barks and resins in the winter when the sap is not running.

Harvesting Techniques

- ❖ Use clean, sharp tools to make precise cuts, ensuring minimal harm to the plant. Harvest in a way that allows the plant to regenerate, taking only part of the plant (e.g., one leaf out of every five) and leaving plenty for wildlife and future growth. Please see our Chapter 3 and Chapter 4 guide for more in depth information on harvesting techniques for each plant you will encounter along your journey.

- ❖ Be mindful of your impact on the surrounding area, avoiding trampling other plants or disturbing wildlife habitats.

Post-Harvest Processing

- ❖ Process your foraged items as soon as possible to preserve their magical and medicinal qualities. Drying, tincturing, or infusing in oil are common methods that maintain the potency of the plants.

- ❖ Store your foraged goods in cool, dark places, in properly labeled containers, to extend their shelf life and retain their effectiveness.

By aligning our foraging practices with the seasonal rhythms of Appalachia and adhering to best practices that honor the land and its spirits, we foster a sustainable relationship with the natural world. This respectful engagement ensures that the ancient art of foraging continues to thrive, weaving the wisdom of the past with the practices of the present, and preserving the sacred dance of humanity and nature for generations to come.

CONCLUDING THOUGHTS

As we draw the curtains on Chapter 2, "Ethical Foraging and Harvesting," we stand at the threshold of a deeper understanding and respect for the bountiful yet delicate tapestry of Appalachian nature. This chapter has not only guided us through the seasonal rhythms and the rich palette of herbs, resins, and woods that the mountains offer but has also grounded us in the foundational ethics of sustainable foraging—a practice that nurtures both the land and our connection to it.

Foraging, as we've explored, is far more than the mere act of gathering; it is a sacred dialogue with the land, a testament to the interdependence of all life. It is a practice steeped in respect, humility, and gratitude, reflecting a deep acknowledgment of the land's generosity and the responsibility we bear to tread lightly upon it.

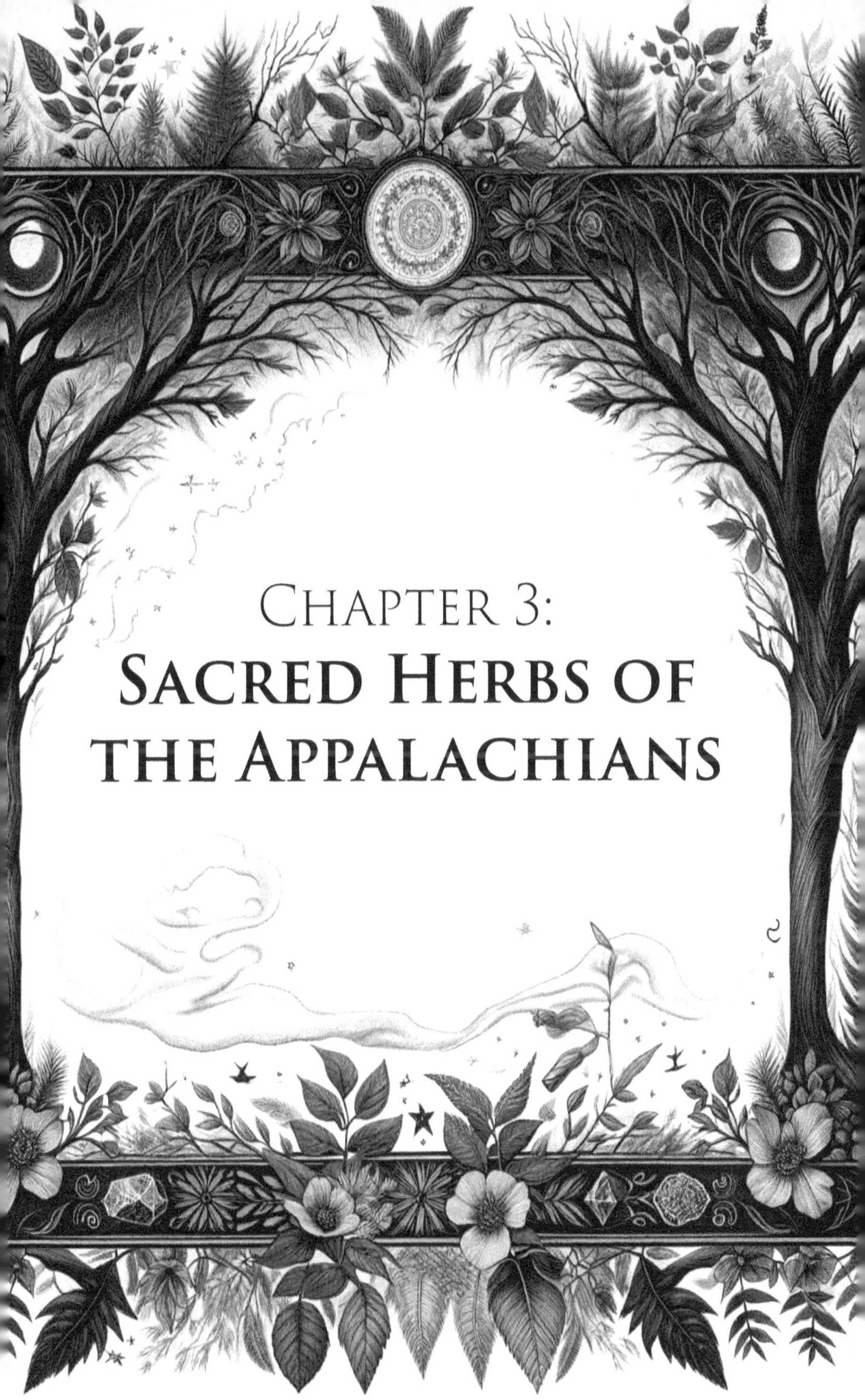

Chapter 3:
Sacred Herbs of the Appalachians

DETAILED PROFILES OF HERBS COMMONLY USED IN APPALACHIAN SMUDGING AND INCENSE

I n the heart of Appalachia, where the ancient mountains whisper secrets to those who know how to listen, the land is lush with a green tapestry of herbs, each carrying its own story, magic, and wisdom. This chapter, "Sacred Herbs of the Appalachians," invites you on a journey through the verdant valleys and mist-shrouded hills, exploring the herbs that are the backbone of local smudging and incense practices, delving into their mystical properties, and uncovering the rich folklore that surrounds them.

Our exploration begins with a selection of herbs that are deeply woven into the fabric of Appalachian magic. Each herb, from the purifying sage to the dream-inducing mugwort and the sweet, sacred sweetgrass, holds a key to unlocking the ancient practices of this region.

SPRING HERBS FOR SMUDGING AND INCENSE IN APPALACHIA

Spring in Appalachia heralds the arrival of potent herbs ideal for smudging and incense rituals. Each herb, with its unique properties and lore, enriches the tapestry of local magical practices. Let's explore the profiles of bloodroot, goldenrod, mugwort, and wild ginger, delving into their identification, harvesting, magical uses, and the folklore that surrounds them.

Bloodroot (Sanguinaria canadensis)

Identification: Bloodroot emerges in early spring, recognizable by its singular, lobed leaf wrapped around a single white flower with numerous yellow stamens at the center. The plant gets its name from the bright red-orange sap within its stems and roots.

Harvesting: Harvest bloodroot carefully and sparingly, as it is a potent plant and should be used with respect. The root is typically harvested when the plant is in bloom.

Post-Harvest: The roots should be cleaned gently and dried thoroughly before use. The red sap can be used as a natural dye in ritual crafts.

Magical Properties and Uses: Bloodroot is used in protective and purification rituals, often added to smudging blends to create a barrier against negative energies. It is also used in spells for fostering new beginnings and healing.

Folklore and Stories: Appalachian lore often portrays bloodroot as a powerful guardian herb, with stories suggesting that carrying a piece of the root can ward off evil spirits and protect against hexes.

Goldenrod (Solidago spp.)

Identification: Goldenrod starts its bloom in late spring, continuing into fall. It is recognized by its tall, slender stems and bright yellow, plume-like flower clusters.

Harvesting: The aerial parts, particularly the flowers, are harvested when the plant is in full bloom, typically in late summer to early fall.

Post-Harvest: The harvested flowers and leaves should be dried and can then be used in incense blends or burned directly as smudge sticks.

Magical Properties and Uses: Goldenrod is associated with divination and is believed to enhance intuitive abilities when used in smudging rituals. It is also used for prosperity spells and to invite positive outcomes.

Folklore and Stories: Goldenrod is imbued with tales of good fortune and finding one's path. Appalachian stories tell of goldenrod pointing the way to hidden treasures and revealing the future when used in divination.

Mugwort (Artemisia vulgaris)

Identification: Mugwort has deeply lobed, dark green leaves with silvery undersides and small reddish or pale purple flowers that appear in dense clusters along its stem in late spring to early summer.

Harvesting: Harvest mugwort leaves and flowering tops in the morning when their aromatic oils are most potent. Mugwort is best harvested just before or during flowering.

Post-Harvest: Dry the harvested plant material thoroughly before using it in smudging sticks or incense blends. Mugwort can also be used fresh in some rituals.

Magical Properties and Uses: Mugwort is renowned for its properties related to dreams, psychic abilities, and protection during astral travel. It is a staple in smudging rituals for purification and to facilitate spiritual journeys.

Folklore and Stories: Mugwort is steeped in Appalachian and broader folklore as a witch's herb, with legends highlighting its ability to open the third eye, protect travelers in the night, and reveal secrets in dreams.

Wild Ginger (Asarum canadense)

Identification: Wild ginger is recognized by its heart-shaped leaves and the small, bell-shaped flowers that hide beneath them, close to the ground. The flowers are reddish-brown, blending with the leaf litter.

Harvesting: The roots of wild ginger are harvested, but given the plant's subtle presence and ecological role, harvesting should be minimal and respectful.

Post-Harvest: Clean and dry the roots carefully. They can be used in powdered form in incense blends or carried as a protective talisman.

Magical Properties and Uses: Wild ginger is used in Appalachian magic for attracting love, stimulating passion, and as a protective charm against negative energies.

Folklore and Stories: Wild ginger is often associated with forest spirits and earth magic in Appalachian tales. It is said to be a favorite of woodland fae and is used in rituals to communicate with nature spirits.

As we connect with these spring herbs through foraging, crafting, and ritual, let us do so with reverence for their wisdom and the land that nurtures them. May our practices honor the traditions and spirits of Appalachia, weaving the magic of the earth into our daily lives.

SUMMER HERBS FOR SMUDGING AND INCENSE IN APPALACHIA

The verdant abundance of summer in Appalachia brings with it a rich array of herbs, each blooming under the long, sunlit days. These herbs, cherished for their aromatic qualities and profound magical properties, play a central role in the region's smudging and incense traditions. Let's explore the summer collection, focusing on identification, harvesting, magical uses, and the folklore woven into their essence.

Bee Balm (Monarda spp.)

Identification: Bee Balm is known for its vibrant red, pink, purple, or white flowers, which form unique, spiky heads. Its leaves are lanceolate and fragrant when crushed.

Harvesting: Harvest the leaves and flowers in full bloom, typically in mid to late summer.

Post-Harvest: Dry the leaves and flowers for use in incense blends or burn them directly for smudging.

Magical Properties and Uses: Bee Balm is used in magic for love, healing, and attracting beneficial spirits or pollinators. It's believed to soothe tensions and promote understanding.

Folklore and Stories: Appalachian lore often celebrates Bee Balm for its strong protective and loving energies, with tales suggesting it's a favorite of hummingbirds and bees, symbolizing joy and sweetness in life.

Chamomile (Matricaria chamomilla)

Identification: Chamomile features daisy-like flowers with white petals surrounding a yellow disc. The leaves are feathery and light green.

Harvesting: Pick the flowers when they are fully open, under the full sun, to capture their essence.

Post-Harvest: Dry the flowers for use in teas, incense blends, or as part of smudging rituals.

Magical Properties and Uses: Chamomile is renowned for its calming, purifying, and protective properties, making it a gentle yet powerful addition to smudging rituals.

Folklore and Stories: In Appalachian tradition, chamomile is believed to attract abundance and to be a balm for restless spirits, bringing peace and prosperity to the home.

Elderflower (Sambucus spp.)

Identification: Elderflower comes from the Elder tree, featuring small, creamy-white flowers clustered in umbels. The tree has compound leaves with serrated leaflets.

Harvesting: Collect the flower heads in late spring to early summer, just as they fully bloom and before the berries form.

Post-Harvest: Use the flowers fresh in infusions or dry them for later use in incense and smudging blends.

Magical Properties and Uses: Elderflower is used for protection, healing, and prosperity. It's believed to ward off negative energy and invite in a deeper spiritual connection.

Folklore and Stories: Elder is steeped in lore, often considered a sacred tree. It's said that an Elder Mother spirit resides within the tree, protecting and blessing those who show her respect.

Hyssop (Hyssopus officinalis)

Identification: Hyssop is a small shrub with narrow, pointed leaves and spikes of blue, pink, or white flowers.

Harvesting: Harvest the leaves and flowers in the summer when the plant is in full bloom.

Post-Harvest: Dry the harvested plant material for use in protective and purifying incense blends.

Magical Properties and Uses: Known for its strong purifying and protective properties, hyssop is often used in smudging rituals to cleanse a space or individual of negative influences.

Folklore and Stories: Hyssop has biblical associations with purification and cleansing, which carry over into Appalachian folk magic, where it's used to purify homes and sacred spaces.

Lavender (Lavandula spp.)

Identification: Lavender is distinguished by its small, tubular, purple flowers arranged in dense spikes atop long stems, with narrow, lance-shaped leaves.

Harvesting: Cut the flower spikes in the early morning after the dew has evaporated but before the sun is fully high.

Post-Harvest: Hang the spikes to dry in a cool, dark place for use in smudging sticks or as loose incense.

Magical Properties and Uses: Lavender is used for peace, relaxation, and protection in smudging rituals. It's believed to induce tranquility, promote sleep, and attract loving energies.

Folklore and Stories: In Appalachian and broader folklore, lavender is said to protect against the evil eye and to ensure fidelity. It's often placed in sachets for peace and restful sleep.

Rosemary (Rosmarinus officinalis)

Identification: Rosemary has needle-like, dark green leaves that are highly aromatic, with small, blue to light purple flowers.

Harvesting: Harvest the sprigs in the morning to capture the essential oils at their peak.

Post-Harvest: Dry the sprigs for later use in cooking, smudging, or as part of incense blends.

Magical Properties and Uses: Rosemary is associated with remembrance, protection, and purification. It's used in smudging rituals to cleanse, protect, and invigorate the space or person.

Folklore and Stories: Appalachian tales often mention rosemary at weddings and funerals, symbolizing remembrance. It's also used in folk medicine for its myriad health benefits.

Sagebrush (Artemisia tridentata)

Identification: Sagebrush, distinct from common sage, features silver-gray leaves with three lobed tips and a strong, pungent aroma.

Harvesting: Collect the leaves, preferably before the plant blooms, to ensure the strongest potency for smudging.

Post-Harvest: Dry the leaves thoroughly before using them in smudging bundles or loose incense.

Magical Properties and Uses: Sagebrush is used for cleansing and purifying, similar to white sage, but with its own unique energy that some find more grounding and less intense.

Folklore and Stories: In many Native American traditions, sagebrush is used for cleansing and healing, a practice adopted into Appalachian folk magic, where it's valued for its strong purifying properties.

Solomon's Seal (Polygonatum spp.)

Identification: Solomon's Seal is characterized by its arching stems, from which hang small, bell-shaped, white or greenish flowers. The leaves are oval and alternate along the stem.

Harvesting: The roots are the most commonly used part and should be harvested with care, as this plant is considered sacred by many and should be used respectfully.

Post-Harvest: Clean and dry the roots carefully; they can be powdered for use in incense blends.

Magical Properties and Uses: Solomon's Seal is used for protection, healing, and exorcising negative energies. It's also believed to aid in sealing spells and making spiritual pacts.

Folklore and Stories: The name "Solomon's Seal" is said to come from the impression on the root that resembles the seal of King Solomon, symbolizing wisdom and protection.

Spicebush (Lindera benzoin)

Identification: Spicebush is a deciduous shrub with aromatic, light green leaves and small, yellow flowers that appear before the leaves in early spring.

Harvesting: The leaves and twigs can be harvested throughout the summer; the berries, which appear in late summer to fall, are also aromatic and can be used.

Post-Harvest: Dry the leaves, twigs, and berries for use in incense blends, where they add a spicy, citrus-like aroma.

Magical Properties and Uses: Spicebush is used in Appalachian magic for cleansing, protection, and bringing prosperity. It's believed to "spice up" spells, adding power and speed to their manifestation.

Folklore and Stories: Appalachian folklore holds spicebush in high regard as a plant of protection and prosperity, with stories of its use to ward off evil and attract wealth.

Sweetgrass (Hierochloe odorata)

Identification: Sweetgrass is notable for its long, slender, bright green leaves and distinctive sweet, vanilla-like scent, particularly when dried and braided.

Harvesting: Harvest sweetgrass by braiding the leaves while still attached to the root, then cutting the braid to allow for regrowth.

Post-Harvest: Dry the braids for use in smudging, where they are burned to produce a sweet, uplifting smoke.

Magical Properties and Uses: Sweetgrass is used for purification and attracting positive spirits. It's often burned after sage in smudging ceremonies to bring in positive energy.

Folklore and Stories: Sweetgrass is considered a sacred plant in many Native American cultures, a belief that has permeated Appalachian folk traditions. It's said to carry prayers to the Creator and to invite the presence of good spirits.

Wild Bergamot (Monarda fistulosa)

Identification: Wild Bergamot, or Bee Balm, sports lavender-pink flowers in dense, round clusters atop square stems. The leaves are lanceolate and fragrant.

Harvesting: Harvest the leaves and flowers in mid to late summer when the plant is in full bloom.

Post-Harvest: Dry the leaves and flowers for use in teas, smudging, or as part of incense blends.

Magical Properties and Uses: Wild Bergamot is used for purification, healing, and to attract prosperity and love. It's believed to clear negative energy and bring balance and peace to a space or individual.

Folklore and Stories: Appalachian lore often features Wild Bergamot in tales of love and healing, with the plant used by traditional healers to soothe the mind and spirit.

Yarrow (Achillea millefolium)

Identification: Yarrow is easily recognized by its feathery, finely divided leaves and clusters of small, white to pinkish flowers.

Harvesting: Collect the flowering tops in the summer when the plant is in full bloom, choosing vibrant, healthy specimens.

Post-Harvest: Dry the flowers and leaves for use in smudging sticks or loose incense, where they lend their protective and healing energies.

Magical Properties and Uses: Yarrow is a powerful herb for protection, courage, and love. It's used in smudging to purify and to create a barrier against negative influences.

Folklore and Stories: In Appalachian and wider folklore, yarrow is associated with ancient warriors and healers alike, believed to staunch wounds and protect against evil. It's also thought to foster love and friendship.

As we embrace the lush growth and vibrant life of summer in Appalachia, let us honor the herbs that offer their gifts for our smudging and incense rituals. May we harvest with respect, use with intention,

and always remember the rich tapestry of folklore and tradition that connects us to these plants and to the land itself.

FALL HERBS FOR SMUDGING AND INCENSE IN APPALACHIA

As the Appalachian landscape quietly shifts from the vibrant tableau of summer to the more subdued and earthy tones of fall, certain plants come into their own, offering their energies for smudging and incense. This season of transition and preparation for the winter ahead brings forth herbs like angelica, Indian pipe, white sage, and wild yam, each with profound spiritual significance and use in traditional practices. Let's delve into their profiles, exploring their identification, harvesting methods, magical uses, and the folklore that imbues them with mystical power.

Angelica (Angelica spp.)

Identification: Angelica is a towering herb with large, bipinnate leaves and hollow stems that can grow up to 6 feet tall. It bears umbels of tiny white or greenish flowers.

Harvesting: Angelica can be harvested in early spring or fall. The roots, seeds, and leaves are all used but harvest the roots either when the plant is dormant in early spring or after the seeds have matured in the fall.

Post-Harvest: Dry the roots and leaves thoroughly before using. The roots can be powdered for incense, and the leaves can be added to smudging bundles.

Magical Properties and Uses: Angelica is known for its protective and healing properties. It's used in smudging rituals to purify a space, invoke protection, and enhance healing energies.

Folklore and Stories: Appalachian folklore regards angelica as a powerful guardian herb, capable of warding off negative energies and spirits. It's said to have been named for the angels, with stories of its divine origin and use in ancient rituals for protection and blessing.

Indian Pipe (Monotropa uniflora)

Identification: Indian Pipe is a unique, ghostly white plant that lacks chlorophyll, making it stand out against the forest floor. It has nodding, bell-shaped flowers on singular, pale stems.

Harvesting: Given its rare and special nature, Indian Pipe should be harvested with great care and respect, and only when abundant. It's typically harvested when in bloom, from late summer to early fall.

Post-Harvest: The entire plant can be dried carefully for use in specialized incense blends, often reserved for significant spiritual rituals.

Magical Properties and Uses: Indian Pipe is used for meditation, transcending the physical realm, and connecting with spiritual energies due to its ethereal appearance and nature.

Folklore and Stories: In Appalachian lore, Indian Pipe is often associated with the spirit world, seen as a bridge between the living and the spirits. Its unusual ghostly white form is said to embody purity and the presence of spirit guides.

White Sage (Salvia apiana)

Identification: White Sage is characterized by its silvery-green leaves that are thick, leathery, and covered in fine hairs, with a potent aromatic scent. It bears white to lavender flowers.

Harvesting: Harvest white sage leaves in the fall when the plant's energies are concentrated in the leaves. Cut the stems with care, ensuring not to overharvest from any one plant.

Post-Harvest: Dry the leaves and stems for use in smudging sticks, ensuring they are thoroughly dried to preserve their aromatic properties.

Magical Properties and Uses: White Sage is renowned for its strong purifying and protective properties, commonly used in smudging rituals to cleanse spaces, objects, and individuals of negative energy.

Folklore and Stories: Though not native to Appalachia and more closely associated with Native American traditions of the Southwest, white sage has been adopted into modern smudging practices widely, including in Appalachian rituals, respected for its powerful cleansing energy.

Wild Yam (Dioscorea villosa)

Identification: Wild Yam is a climbing vine with heart-shaped, alternate leaves and small, drooping greenish-white flowers. The tuberous roots are the most significant part of the plant.

Harvesting: The roots of Wild Yam can be harvested in the fall when the plant's energies have returned to the earth. Dig carefully around the plant to unearth the tuberous roots.

Post-Harvest: Clean and dry the roots thoroughly before use. They can be powdered for inclusion in incense blends.

Magical Properties and Uses: Wild Yam is used in rituals for fertility and to ease transitions, embodying the cycles of change and renewal. It's also associated with soothing and grounding energies in magical practices.

Folklore and Stories: In Appalachian herbal medicine and folklore, Wild Yam is revered for its nurturing and supportive properties, often used by midwives and healers. It carries tales of feminine wisdom, motherhood, and the cycles of life and death.

As we gather these fall herbs, let us do so with mindfulness and gratitude for the abundance the earth offers. May our practices honor the changing seasons

TIPS FOR GROWING YOUR OWN MAGICAL HERBS WITH AN APPALACHIAN TWIST

Cultivating a garden of magical herbs in the rich soil of the Appalachian region is not just about planting seeds; it's about weaving a tapestry of tradition, wisdom, and respect for the land. Each herb in your garden carries a story, a spirit, and a power that can be nurtured and grown with the right care and intentions. Here, we delve into the art of growing your own magical herbs, infusing each step with the unique essence of Appalachian wisdom.

Cultivation Tips for Appalachian Herb Gardens

Soil Preparation

The foundation of any garden is its soil. Most magical herbs thrive in well-drained, fertile soil rich in organic matter. Begin by testing your soil to understand its composition and pH level. Many herbs prefer a neutral to slightly acidic pH. Amend your soil with compost or aged manure to improve fertility and structure, particularly if you're working with the clay-heavy soils common in parts of Appalachia.

Sunlight and Water Requirements

Most magical herbs, such as sage, lavender, and chamomile, require full sun, meaning at least six hours of direct sunlight daily. However, some, like wild ginger and Indian pipe, thrive in the dappled shade of woodland gardens, mirroring their native habitats beneath the Appalachian canopy.

Water needs vary among herbs. While lavender and sage prefer drier conditions, mimicking their native Mediterranean climate, plants like bee balm and wild bergamot thrive with more moisture. Implement rainwater harvesting techniques to provide your garden with a natural water source, and always water at the base of the plants to prevent fungal diseases.

Organic Pest Control

Maintaining the purity of your magical herbs means avoiding chemical pesticides. Use organic pest control methods like neem oil, diatomaceous earth, or insecticidal soaps. Introduce beneficial insects, such as ladybugs and lacewings, to naturally control pest populations. Planting garlic, chives, or marigolds around your herb garden can also help repel unwanted pests.

Appalachian Gardening Wisdom

Planting by the Moon Phases

Appalachian folklore holds deep knowledge about planting by the moon phases. The waxing moon, from new to full, is believed to be the best time for planting herbs that bear fruit above ground, as the increasing moonlight encourages leafy growth. The waning moon, from full to new, is favored for planting root crops, as the decreasing moonlight draws energy downward into the earth.

Companion Planting

Companion planting is a practice deeply rooted in Appalachian gardening traditions, where certain plants are grown together for mutual benefit. For instance, planting chamomile near other herbs can increase their oil content, enhancing their magical properties. Lavender and rosemary, when planted together, support each other's growth and repel common pests, creating a harmonious and protective garden environment.

Speaking to Plants and Blessings

Appalachian lore suggests that speaking to your plants or singing to them can encourage their growth. This practice is not just about the physical vibrations but about the intention and energy you share. Incorporate blessings or prayers into your gardening routine, asking for the spirits of the land and the ancestors to bless your garden with abundance and health.

Harvesting and Blessing

Ethical Harvesting

Harvest your herbs with respect and gratitude, acknowledging the gifts they offer. Always harvest in the morning after the dew has evaporated but before the full heat of the sun, when the plants' oils are at their

peak. Use sharp, clean scissors or pruners to make clean cuts, and never take more than one-third of the plant to ensure its continued vitality.

Harvesting by Moon Phases and Times of Day

The timing of your harvest can enhance the magical properties of your herbs. Harvesting leafy herbs under a waxing moon can capture the essence of growth and expansion, while harvesting roots under a waning moon can tap into energies of grounding and protection. Consider also the planetary hours; for instance, harvesting during Venus hours can imbue herbs like rosemary and lavender with stronger love and healing vibrations.

Rituals and Blessings

Performing a small ritual or offering a blessing during harvesting honors the spirit of the plant and the land. This can be as simple as taking a moment to ground and center yourself, offering a verbal thank you, or leaving a small offering of water, organic fertilizer, or a stone at the base of the plant. Some may choose to recite a traditional blessing or prayer, or simply to express gratitude in their heart for the plant's sacrifice and gifts.

In cultivating your magical herb garden with these practices, you're not just growing plants; you're nurturing a sacred space, a living altar to the earth and the spirits that dwell within it. Each herb you tend with love and respect becomes a powerful ally in your magical and spiritual practices, infused with the deep-rooted energies of the Appalachian lands.

Concluding Thoughts

As we close Chapter 3 of "Sacred Smoke and Mountain Spirits," we find ourselves deeply rooted in the verdant world of Appalachian herbs, each with its own story, spirit, and ancient wisdom. Through the detailed profiles of these sacred plants, we've journeyed into the heart of traditional smudging and incense-making practices, uncovering the layers of magic and folklore that intertwine with the everyday and the mystical in Appalachian life.

This chapter has not only served as a guide to the potent herbs that grace these ancient mountains but also as an invitation to engage with them in a way that honors their spirit and the land that nourishes them. From the protective embrace of sage and the dreamy whispers of mugwort to the loving touch of lavender and the profound grounding of wild ginger, each herb offers a key to unlocking the deeper connections between us, the earth, and the unseen forces that animate our world.

The cultivation tips, woven with threads of Appalachian gardening wisdom, provide a practical pathway to integrating these sacred plants into our lives. Planting by the moon's phases, embracing companion planting, and engaging in the timeless practice of speaking to plants remind us that gardening is not just an act of cultivation but a sacred dialogue. This dialogue, enriched with blessings and rituals of harvesting, transforms our gardens into living altars, where every leaf and root is a testament to the cycle of giving and receiving that defines our existence.

As we step forward from this chapter, let us carry with us the reverence for the land that Appalachian traditions teach. Let the herbs we grow and forage not just be ingredients for our rituals but cherished allies in our spiritual journey, each with a story to tell and a blessing to offer. May our practices of smudging and incense-making be imbued with the profound respect and love we hold for these plant beings and the ancient mountains they call home.

In "Sacred Smoke and Mountain Spirits," we are not merely observers of tradition but active participants in the living tapestry of Appalachian magic. As we blend, burn, and bless with these sacred herbs, let us do so with the intention to heal, protect, and connect, weaving our

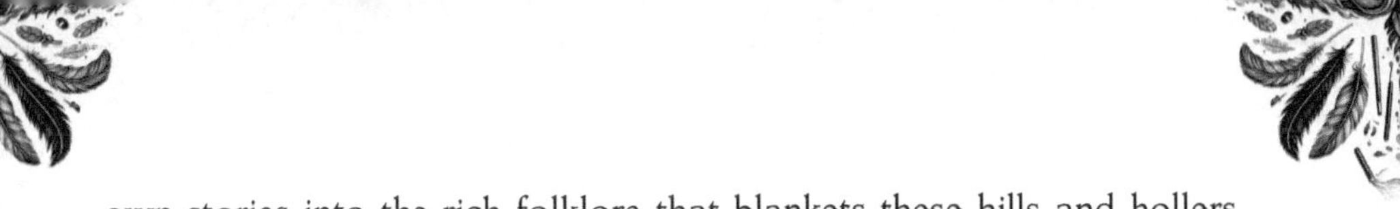

own stories into the rich folklore that blankets these hills and hollers. Our journey through the world of Appalachian smoke magic is a path of discovery, where every herb, every ritual, and every breath of sacred smoke draws us closer to the heartbeat of the earth and the whispers of the ancestors who walked these paths before us.

Chapter 4:
Trees and Resins of Power

Exploring the Magical Uses of Appalachian Trees and Resins in Smoke Magic

In the heart of Appalachia, where ancient mountains whisper secrets through the leaves of towering trees and hidden resins hold the essence of the earth, lies a wellspring of natural magic. "Trees and Resins of Power," the fourth chapter of "Sacred Smoke and Mountain Spirits," invites us to explore the sacred bond between humans and the forest, revealing the profound magical uses of Appalachian trees and their resins in the venerable art of smoke magic.

Exploring the Magical Uses of Appalachian Trees and Resins in Smoke Magic

Tree Profiles

In this verdant expanse, each tree—be it the mighty Oak, the whispering Pine, or the resilient Cedar—carries within it a unique spirit, an ancient wisdom, and a potent magic. The Oak, revered for its strength and endurance, offers leaves and acorns that, when burned, provide grounding and protective energies, creating a stable foundation for any magical work. The Pine, with its evergreen branches and sappy resin, is a beacon of purification and illumination, clearing spaces of negativity and filling them with vibrant, renewing energy.

The Birch, with its white, papery bark and slender leaves, is a symbol of new beginnings and regeneration. Birch bark, when added to smudging blends, can facilitate personal transformation and cleanse spaces of old energies, making way for the new. The Cedar, ancient and majestic, offers both fragrant wood and resin, known for their properties of cleansing, protection, and the invocation of spiritual aid.

Resin Magic

Resins, the lifeblood of many Appalachian trees, are a focal point of smoke magic. The golden droplets of Pine resin, the aromatic beads of Spruce, and the rich, fragrant sap of Cedar are all harvested with reverence for their powerful cleansing, healing, and protective properties.

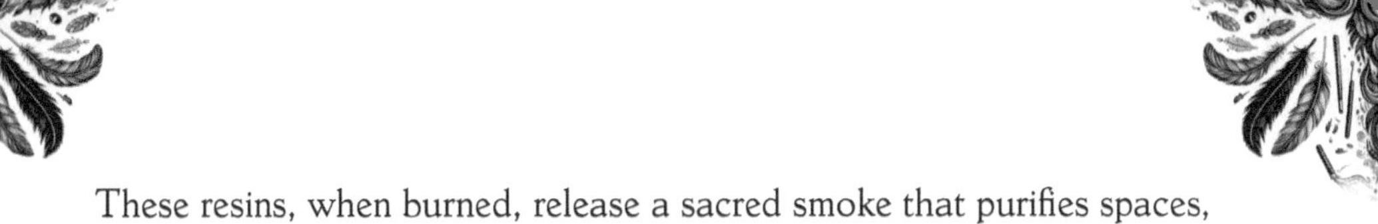

These resins, when burned, release a sacred smoke that purifies spaces, objects, and auras, carrying prayers and intentions to the spirit world.

Folklore Associated with Specific Trees and How to Respectfully Harvest Tree Products for Magical Use

Tree Lore

The trees of Appalachia are steeped in folklore, each species entwined with tales that speak of their sacred nature. The Oak is often seen as the doorway to other realms, a meeting place for the old gods and a guardian of ancient wisdom. Pine trees are said to house spirits within their resin-filled trunks, whispering secrets to those who listen closely. Cedar is believed to be a bridge between heaven and earth, its fragrant smoke carrying messages to the ancestors.

These stories, passed down through generations, imbue the trees with a sacred significance, transforming the act of harvesting their leaves, bark, wood, or resin into a deeply spiritual practice.

Ethical Harvesting Practices

Harvesting from these venerable beings is an act that requires respect, mindfulness, and gratitude. Before taking anything, one should always communicate with the tree spirit, seeking permission and expressing the purpose of the harvest. Offerings of water, natural fertilizers, or a strand of hair can be made to the tree as a token of gratitude and reciprocity.

When collecting leaves or bark, use clean, sharp tools to make precise cuts, ensuring the tree's swift healing. Resins should be gathered in small amounts, allowing the tree to maintain its natural defenses against pests and diseases.

Conservation Awareness

As stewards of the land, it is our duty to approach the harvesting of tree products with a conservation-minded spirit. This means being acutely aware of the impact of our actions on the forest ecosystem and ensuring that our practices contribute to the health and vitality of these ancient woodlands. It involves educating ourselves and others about the importance of preserving these natural habitats, not only for their magical and spiritual significance but also for their crucial role in sustaining life on our planet.

In weaving together the rich tapestry of magical uses, folklore, and ethical harvesting practices associated with the trees and resins of Appalachia, Chapter 4 serves as a reminder of our deep connection to the natural world. It calls us to walk the forest paths with reverence, to listen to the whispered wisdom of the leaves and branches, and to honor the sacred dance of giving and receiving that sustains us all. As practitioners of Appalachian smoke magic, we are keepers of this ancient bond, guardians of the secrets held within the heartwood, and celebrants of the sacred smoke that rises from our altars, uniting heaven, earth, and the spirit within.

TREES FOR SMUDGING AND INCENSE IN APPALACHIA

Birch

Identification: Birch trees are recognizable by their distinctive white or silver bark that often peels in horizontal strips. The leaves are generally small, oval to triangular, with serrated edges. Birches are known for their slender trunks and graceful branches.

Harvesting: Birch bark can be harvested year-round, but it's essential to do so responsibly to avoid damaging the tree. Only take bark from fallen branches or trees, never from the living trunk. Birch leaves can be gathered in spring and early summer when they are most vibrant.

Post-Harvest: Dry the leaves and small pieces of bark in a shaded, well-ventilated area until they are brittle. Store in a cool, dry place until ready to use for smudging or incense.

Resins in Smoke Magic: While birch is not as resinous as pine or cedar, the bark, when burned, releases a light, sweet fragrance conducive to purification and protection rituals.

Folklore: In various cultures, including Appalachian folklore, birch is seen as a tree of new beginnings and protection. It is often associated with the goddess Brigid and is used in May Day celebrations. Birch branches are traditionally used to craft besoms (ritual brooms), symbolizing a clean sweep of old energies to make way for the new.

Cedar (Juniperus virginiana)

Identification: Cedar, specifically the Eastern Red Cedar, features dense, dark-green to blue-green foliage with a pyramid shape. Its leaves transition from needle-like on young trees to scale-like on mature trees. The bark is fibrous and reddish-brown, peeling in narrow strips.

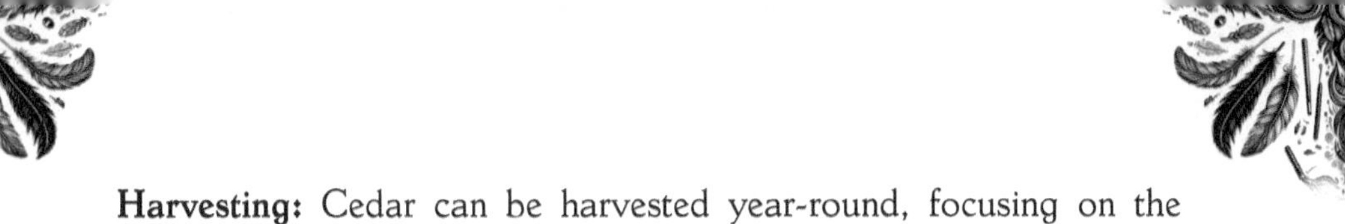

Harvesting: Cedar can be harvested year-round, focusing on the leaves (needles) and small twigs. Use clean, sharp pruning shears, ensuring not to overharvest from any one tree.

Post-Harvest: Dry the harvested needles and twigs in a cool, dark place with good air circulation. Once dry, they can be bundled for smudging or used loose in incense blends.

Resins in Smoke Magic: Cedar resin is valued for its purifying properties in smoke magic. Although less commonly harvested than pine resin, it can be collected from natural exudations on the tree and used in incense for cleansing and protection.

Folklore: Cedar is revered in both Appalachian and Native American traditions as a powerful guardian and purifier. It is believed to house good spirits and is often used in cleansing rituals to ward off negative influences.

Juniper (Juniperus spp.)

Identification: Junipers are characterized by their sharp, needle-like leaves and blue or black berry-like cones. The bark is usually gray or brown and may peel in thin strips or sheets.

Harvesting: Harvest juniper berries in late summer to early fall when ripe, and branches can be harvested year-round. Use clean, sharp scissors or pruners, taking care not to overharvest.

Post-Harvest: Dry the berries and branches in a cool, dark place. Berries may take several weeks to dry fully and can be used whole or crushed in incense blends, while branches can be used fresh or dried for smudging.

Resins in Smoke Magic: Juniper resin, though not as prevalent as in pine or cedar, carries protective and purifying properties. It can be used in incense blends for its crisp, cleansing scent.

Folklore: Juniper is steeped in protection and health lore, often used to ward off evil spirits and illnesses. In Appalachian folklore, juniper branches are hung over doorways or burned to purify homes and protect their inhabitants.

Oak

Identification: Oaks are mighty trees with broad, lobed leaves and a rugged, deeply grooved bark. They produce distinctive acorns, which are often a key identifying feature.

Harvesting: Oak leaves and acorns can be harvested in the fall. Use clean, sharp tools to gather leaves, and pick acorns directly from the ground or the tree.

Post-Harvest: Dry the leaves in a shaded, well-ventilated area. Acorns can be used as is or dried for longer storage. Both can be incorporated into incense blends for their strong, grounding energy.

Resins in Smoke Magic: While oaks are not typically known for their resin, the wood and leaves, especially when oak galls are present, can be used in smoke magic for grounding, strength, and protection.

Folklore: Oak is a symbol of strength, endurance, and wisdom in many traditions, including Appalachian lore. It is often associated with thunder gods and was used in ancient times for its protective qualities.

Pine (Pinus spp.)

Identification: Pine trees are known for their long, needle-like leaves grouped in clusters and their woody cones. The bark varies among species but often features deep furrows with a reddish-brown hue.

Harvesting: Pine needles, bark, and resin can be collected year-round. For needles and twigs, use clean, sharp shears, being careful not to overharvest. Resin can be collected from natural exudations on the bark.

Post-Harvest: Dry needles and twigs in a shaded area with good air circulation. Pine resin can be used as is in incense for its aromatic and purifying properties.

Resins in Smoke Magic: Pine resin is highly valued for its potent cleansing and protective properties in smoke magic, ideal for purifying spaces, objects, and auras.

Folklore: Pine is revered for its resilience and life-affirming qualities. In Appalachian and broader folklore, it's associated with health, prosperity, and protection, often used in winter solstice celebrations.

Spruce

Identification: Spruce trees are known for their conical shape, short, sharp needles that attach individually to the branches, and small, hanging cones. The needles of a spruce are four-sided, allowing them to be rolled between your fingers, which is a distinguishing feature from fir trees. The bark tends to be rough and scaly.

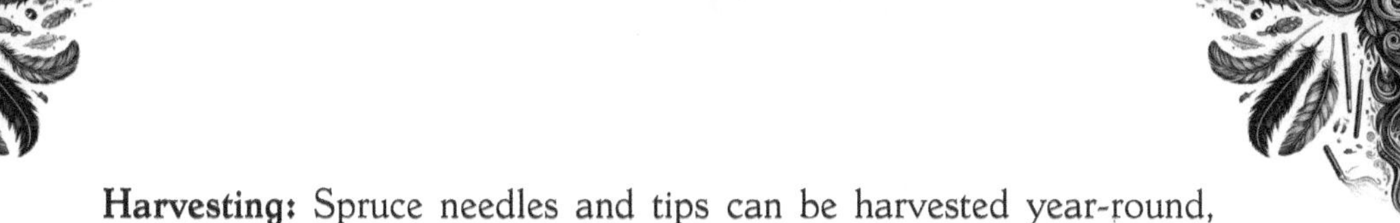

Harvesting: Spruce needles and tips can be harvested year-round, but the best time is in late spring when the new growth, or "spruce tips," emerge. These are softer and have a higher concentration of vitamins and a more pleasant flavor. Use clean, sharp scissors or pruners to snip the tips or needles, being mindful not to overharvest from any single tree.

Post-Harvest: Dry the spruce tips or needles in a cool, dark place with good air circulation. Once dried, they can be used whole or ground into a powder for incense blends. The tips are especially valued for their bright, fresh scent and can be used in a variety of medicinal and culinary applications as well.

Resins in Smoke Magic: Like pine and cedar, spruce trees produce a resin that can be used in smoke magic. Spruce resin has a clean, forest-like fragrance when burned and is used for its purifying and protective properties. It can be collected from the tree where it naturally exudes and then allowed to harden.

Folklore: Spruce trees hold a significant place in folklore across various cultures, including Appalachian traditions. They are often associated with resilience and the ability to endure harsh conditions, symbolizing persistence and strength. Spruce is also connected to protection and purification rites, with its branches and resin used to cleanse spaces and create protective barriers against negative forces.

CONCLUDING THOUGHTS

As we draw the final leaves of Chapter 4, "Trees and Resins of Power," to a close, we are reminded of the profound connection between the ancient Appalachian forests and the enduring practices of smoke magic that have flourished within this verdant realm. This chapter has served as a gateway into the majestic world of towering cedars, whispering pines, stoic oaks, resilient birches, and the stoic spruce, each offering their unique gifts to the tapestry of Appalachian magical traditions.

Through the exploration of these sacred trees and their potent resins, we've delved into the heart of smoke magic, uncovering the ways in which these natural elements are harnessed to purify, protect, and connect us to the spiritual realms. The rich folklore woven around each tree has illuminated the path, revealing the deep reverence and symbiotic relationship that our ancestors cultivated with these living sentinels of the forest.

The guidance provided on respectful and sustainable harvesting practices serves as a reminder of our responsibility to these guardians of the land. It underscores the importance of approaching each tree with humility and gratitude, recognizing the sacrifice they make in offering parts of themselves for our spiritual work. This ethical approach ensures the continuation of these practices for generations to come, preserving the sacred balance between taking and giving back to the earth.

As we move forward from this chapter, let us carry with us the wisdom of the cedars, the strength of the oaks, the resilience of the pines, the purification of the birches, and the protection of the spruce. May our smudging rituals and incense-making endeavors be infused with the profound energies of these trees, each breath of sacred smoke a prayer of gratitude to the spirits of the forest.

"Trees and Resins of Power" has not only expanded our knowledge of Appalachian smoke magic but has also deepened our connection to the natural world, reminding us of the intricate web of life that sustains us all. As practitioners of this ancient art, we are custodians of a rich heritage, bearers of a sacred flame that lights the way to understanding, healing, and unity with the natural world.

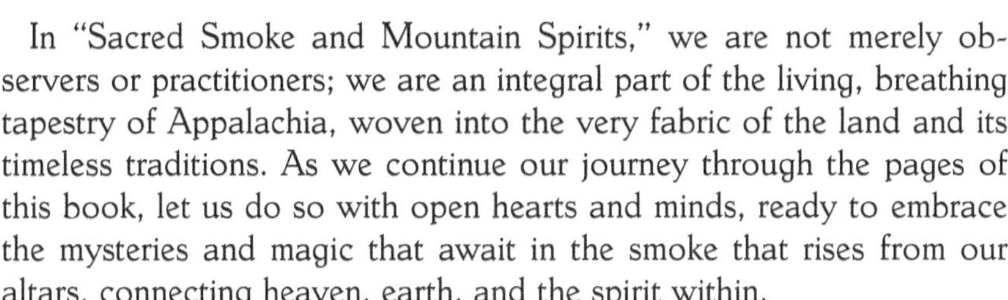

In "Sacred Smoke and Mountain Spirits," we are not merely observers or practitioners; we are an integral part of the living, breathing tapestry of Appalachia, woven into the very fabric of the land and its timeless traditions. As we continue our journey through the pages of this book, let us do so with open hearts and minds, ready to embrace the mysteries and magic that await in the smoke that rises from our altars, connecting heaven, earth, and the spirit within.

Chapter 5:
Crafting Your Incense

STEP-BY-STEP GUIDES TO MAKING LOOSE INCENSE BLENDS, STICKS, AND CONES USING APPALACHIAN INGREDIENTS

In the heart of Appalachia, where the air is laced with the earthy scents of the forest and the ancient wisdom of the mountains, the art of crafting incense is a sacred practice that connects us to the land, its spirits, and our deepest intentions. This chapter invites you on a journey to explore the traditional craft of making incense using the rich palette of Appalachian ingredients, guiding you through the creation of loose incense blends, sticks, and cones, each imbued with the magic of this storied region.

Loose Incense Blends: The Foundation of Smoke Magic

Loose incense blends form the cornerstone of Appalachian smoke magic, a potent alchemy of herbs, resins, and woods that, when burned, release their energies into the air, carrying prayers and intentions to the spirit realm. Crafting your blend begins with understanding the properties and correspondences of local ingredients, allowing you to tailor your incense to specific magical purposes, be it for protection, purification, healing, or communion with the ancestral spirits.

Selecting Your Ingredients: Begin by choosing your base ingredients, which might include the cleansing leaves of white sage or the grounding bark of cedar. To this, add resins like pine for purification or spruce for protection, lending their sticky, aromatic essence to the blend. Consider also the inclusion of fragrant herbs like wild bergamot for relaxation or sweetgrass for attracting positive spirits.

Formulating Your Blend: The art of formulation is as much intuitive as it is practical. Start with a simple base of three ingredients, focusing on your primary intention. For purification, a blend of cedar, pine resin, and lavender can create a purifying and calming smoke. For grounding and protection, consider oak bark, spruce resin, and a touch of mugwort. As you become more familiar with the properties of each ingredient, you can experiment with more complex blends.

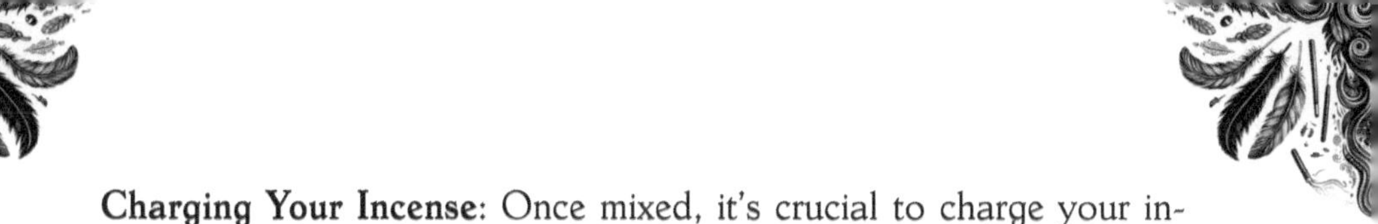

Charging Your Incense: Once mixed, it's crucial to charge your incense with your intention. This can be done through a simple ritual where you hold the incense in your hands, envisioning your intention being absorbed by the blend. You might choose to recite a prayer, chant, or affirmation that encapsulates your desired outcome, imbuing the incense with your personal energy and purpose.

Burning Your Blend: Loose incense is traditionally burned on a charcoal disc placed within a fireproof container. As the smoke rises, visualize your intentions being carried upwards, merging with the universal energies to manifest your desires.

Incense Sticks and Cones: Crafting Personalized Magical Tools

For those who prefer a more portable or controlled burn, crafting your own incense sticks and cones offers a deep dive into the creative and magical aspects of incense making. This process not only allows for a personalized touch but also deepens your connection to the ingredients and their inherent magic.

Creating the Mixture: Begin with a powdered mixture of your chosen herbs, resins, and woods. To bind your incense, you'll need a natural adhesive - makko powder, derived from the bark of the tabu-no-ki tree, is a traditional choice that burns smoothly and evenly. Gradually mix in water until you achieve a pliable dough-like consistency.

Forming Sticks and Cones: For sticks, you might use a bamboo skewer or similar base, rolling a thin layer of the mixture around it and ensuring even thickness. For cones, shape small amounts of the mixture with your fingers, forming a base and a pointed top. Both forms require patience and a gentle touch.

Drying Your Incense: Once shaped, your sticks and cones need to be thoroughly dried to ensure a smooth burn. Place them on wax paper in a dry, warm area away from direct sunlight, turning them occasionally to ensure even drying. This process can take several days to a week, depending on humidity and thickness.

Preserving and Storing Incense: Proper storage is key to maintaining the potency and fragrance of your incense. Once fully dried, store your sticks and cones in airtight containers, preferably in a cool, dark place. Label each batch with the date and ingredients to keep track of your creations.

Through the mindful selection of ingredients, the careful crafting of blends, and the intentional charging of each piece, the incense you create becomes a powerful tool in your magical arsenal. It carries the essence of the Appalachian wilds, the ancestral wisdom of its people, and the personal touch of your hands and heart. As you light your incense, let the sacred smoke envelop you, connecting you to the vast web of life that pulses through these ancient mountains, and to the magic that flows like a hidden stream beneath the surface of all things.

Formulating Intentions and Selecting Corresponding Materials

In the heart of Appalachian incense-making lies the sacred act of intention setting, a practice that imbues your creations with purpose, transforming them into potent tools for ritual and magical work. This subsection delves into the art of aligning your intentions with the natural energies of herbs, resins, and woods, ensuring that every pinch of material and every swirl of smoke carries your desires into the realm of manifestation.

Intention Setting: The Heartbeat of Your Incense

The process of making incense begins long before the physical act of mixing and molding—it starts with intention. Intention is the seed from which the power of your incense grows, guiding its use and defining its potency. Setting a clear intention is akin to plotting a course on a map; it determines the direction and outcome of your magical work.

The Power of Intention: When you set an intention, you are essentially programming your incense with a specific energetic blueprint. This could be as broad as seeking overall protection for your home or as focused as inviting clarity into a difficult decision. The clarity and specificity of your intention directly influence the effectiveness of your incense, acting as a beacon for the energies you wish to attract or repel.

Infusing Intention: To infuse your incense with your intention, take a moment to center and ground yourself before beginning the crafting process. Hold the intention clearly in your mind or, if you prefer, write it down on a piece of paper. As you mix and mold your incense, visualize your intention being absorbed into the materials, imagine the outcome you desire, and feel the emotions associated with its realization. This act of visualization and emotional engagement charges the incense with your personal energy and purpose.

Material Selection: Harmonizing Intentions with Appalachian Botanicals

The natural world is replete with materials that carry their own inherent energies, each resonating with specific intentions. The key to effective incense-making lies in selecting botanicals that align with and amplify your set intentions. Below is a reference guide to assist in matching common intentions with their corresponding Appalachian botanicals and their magical properties.

Reference Table for Intentions and Corresponding Materials

Intention	Botanical	Magical Properties
Purification	Sage (Salvia spp.)	Cleanses spaces and objects of negative energies
Protection	Cedar (Juniperus virginiana)	Acts as a shield against negative forces
Healing	Lavender (Lavandula spp.)	Promotes physical and emotional healing
Love	Wild Rose (Rosa spp.)	Attracts and nurtures loving energies
Prosperity	Birch Bark (Betula spp.)	Invites abundance and new opportunities
Communication	Bee Balm (Monarda spp.)	Enhances clarity and ease in communication
Grounding	Pine Resin (Pinus spp.)	Connects to earth energies, providing stability
Intuition	Mugwort (Artemisia vulgaris)	Opens the third eye, enhancing psychic abilities

Harmonizing Materials with Intentions: Once you have identified the materials that correspond to your intention, consider how they can be combined to enhance the incense's effectiveness. For example, an incense blend crafted for protection might primarily feature cedar but could be bolstered by the inclusion of sage for purification and pine resin for grounding, creating a multi-layered shield of protection.

Respecting the Materials: As you select and work with these Appalachian botanicals, remember to honor their origins and the land that has nurtured them. Acknowledge the spirit of each plant and its

willingness to lend its energy to your work, fostering a relationship of mutual respect and gratitude.

By intertwining the art of intention setting with the mindful selection of resonant materials, your incense-making becomes more than a craft—it becomes a sacred act, a dialogue with the natural world, and a deep expression of your innermost desires and aspirations. Let each herb you crush and each resin you melt be a testament to the power of intention and the magic inherent in the Appalachian wilderness.

APPALACHIAN TWILIGHT INCENSE BLEND

In the serene twilight hours, as shadows dance softly upon the Appalachian landscape and the sky transitions from the vibrant hues of sunset to the deep indigo of night, a sacred ritual unfolds. This Appalachian Twilight Incense Blend is a tribute to these magical moments, capturing the essence of dusk and the tranquil power of the mountains at twilight. It's a blend designed to harmonize with the energies of evening, promoting peace, reflection, and the gentle release of the day's burdens.

Materials Needed:

- **Cedar Tips (Juniperus virginiana)**: Gathered from the majestic Cedar trees, these tips bring protection and grounding, embodying the steadfast spirit of the Appalachians.

- **Lavender Flowers (Lavandula spp.)**: Harvested from the fragrant lavender that adorns the mountain gardens, these flowers add a layer of calm and purification to the blend, soothing the mind and spirit.

- **Sage Leaves (Salvia spp.)**: The sage, with its cleansing properties, acts as a purifier, clearing the space and the aura of any lingering negativity from the day.

- **Pine Resin (Pinus spp.)**: The golden droplets of resin, collected with reverence from the Pine trees, bring a touch of purification and renewal, their rich aroma grounding and uplifting the spirit.

- **A Mortar and Pestle**: To blend and release the energies of the botanicals.

- **A Charcoal Disc and Fireproof Container**: For burning the incense.

Preparation: Choose a quiet spot where the fading light of day meets the emerging stars, a place that resonates with the peaceful solitude of the Appalachian evening. Prepare your space by laying out your materials, letting the tranquility of the twilight envelop you.

Crafting the Blend:

1. **Botanical Harmony**: Begin by placing a small amount of cedar tips into your mortar, grounding yourself in their protective energy. Add lavender flowers next, allowing their calming scent to weave through the blend, followed by crumbled sage leaves for purification.

2. **Resin Alchemy**: With a gentle hand, add small pieces of pine resin to the mixture. The resin, embodying the resilience and renewal of the mountains, adds a rich, purifying smoke to your blend.

3. **Melding Energies**: Using the pestle, gently grind and mix the botanicals and resin together, focusing on your intention for peace, purification, and grounding. As you work, envision the twilight energies of the Appalachians infusing your blend with a serene power.

4. **Invocation of Twilight**: As the blend becomes harmonized, hold the mortar in your hands and whisper an invocation that captures the essence of Appalachian twilights, such as, "With this blend, I call upon the serene twilight, the protective embrace of the cedar, the calm of the lavender, the purity of the sage, and the resilience of the pine. May this smoke carry away the day's burdens, leaving peace and tranquility in its wake."

Using the Incense: Place a charcoal disc in your fireproof container and light it. Once it's glowing, sprinkle a small amount of your Appalachian Twilight Incense Blend onto the disc. As the smoke begins to rise, let it envelop you, carrying away the day's worries and filling the space with a deep, tranquil peace. Reflect on the beauty and serenity of the Appalachian landscape at twilight, allowing it to inspire calm and contemplation.

Closing the Ritual: As the incense burns down and the night deepens, offer a word of thanks to the plants, the land, and the twilight for their gifts. Store any remaining incense blend in an airtight container, keeping it for future evenings when you wish to invoke the peaceful spirit of the Appalachian twilight once again.

APPALACHIAN DAWN INCENSE STICK CRAFTING RITUAL

In the serene hours of dawn, when the first light of the sun kisses the Appalachian peaks and valleys, a time-honored ritual unfolds, weaving the essence of the awakening land into a sacred incense stick. This Appalachian Dawn Incense Stick Crafting Ritual is a celebration of new beginnings, drawing on the rejuvenating energy of the morning to infuse the incense with intentions of renewal, clarity, and invigoration. It harnesses the vibrant energies of Appalachian botanicals, crafting a tool that carries the fresh promise of the dawn.

Materials Needed:

- **Sage (Salvia spp.) Powder**: Symbolizing purification and wisdom, ground from the leaves of sage that carpet the mountain slopes.

- **Pine (Pinus spp.) Resin**: The golden tears of pine trees, collected with reverence, offering protection and grounding.

- **Lavender (Lavandula spp.) Flowers**: The delicate blooms of Appalachian lavender, dried and ground, to bring calm and peace.

- **Makko Powder**: A natural binder derived from the bark of the Thunbergia tree, ensuring the incense stick burns smoothly.

- **Bamboo Sticks**: The base for the incense sticks, representing strength and flexibility.

- **A Mixing Bowl and Spoon**: For blending the botanicals and makko powder.

- **Distilled Water**: To bind the mixture, symbolizing the element of water and its cleansing properties.

Preparation: Greet the dawn in a peaceful spot where the morning's first light can touch you, a place that resonates with the quiet beauty and strength of the Appalachian landscape. Lay out your materials, allowing the fresh energy of the new day to infuse them.

Crafting the Blend:

1. **Botanical Awakening**: Begin by placing sage powder into your mixing bowl, setting your intention for purification and wisdom. Add pine resin for its protective energies, followed by the lavender flowers for a touch of peace and tranquility.

2. **Merging with Makko**: Introduce the makko powder to your botanical blend, ensuring that your incense stick will burn with consistency and grace. The makko not only serves as a binder but also honors the traditional art of incense-making.

3. **Infusion of Intentions**: As you mix the ingredients with distilled water to form a pliable dough, focus on your intentions for the day ahead. With each stir, envision the incense stick illuminating your path with clarity, grounding, and peace.

4. **Shaping New Beginnings**: Gently roll portions of the dough around the bamboo sticks, creating a thin layer of the incense mixture. As you work, imbue each stick with your aspirations for renewal and growth.

Drying and Charging: Place the incense sticks in a cool, airy spot to dry, away from direct sunlight. This process might take a few days. As they dry, imagine the sticks absorbing the potent energies of the dawn, becoming charged with the vibrancy and promise of new beginnings.

Morning Invocation: As the incense sticks dry, greet each new dawn with a simple invocation, such as, "With the light of this new day, I charge these sticks with renewal, clarity, and peace. May they carry the fresh energies of the Appalachian dawn, guiding me with wisdom and grounding me in strength."

Closing the Ritual: Once the incense sticks are fully dried, gather them and offer a word of gratitude to the dawn, the land, and the botanicals that have contributed their essence to your creation. Store the sticks in a cool, dark place until you are ready to use them, each time reigniting the vibrant energies of Appalachian mornings and the intentions set within.

This ritual, deeply rooted in the traditions and natural beauty of Appalachia, offers a way to start each day with purpose and connection to the earth. The incense sticks crafted in the spirit of the Appalachian dawn serve as sacred tools, guiding you through the day with the serene and renewing energies of the morning light.

APPALACHIAN SUNSET INCENSE CONE CRAFTING RITUAL

In the tranquil moments of twilight, as the sun dips below the horizon, painting the Appalachian skies with hues of fiery orange and soft lavender, a sacred ritual takes place. This Appalachian Sunset Incense Cone

Crafting Ritual is an ode to the closing of the day, a time for reflection, gratitude, and the gentle release of all that has transpired. It captures the essence of the evening, utilizing the rich botanicals of the region to create incense cones infused with the calming and grounding energies of the Appalachian dusk.

Materials Needed:

- **Cedar (Juniperus virginiana) Powder**: Ground from the protective boughs of the Cedar, embodying the strength and stability of the mountains.

- **Juniper (Juniperus spp.) Berries**: Dried and ground, these berries bring purification and protection, echoing the whispers of the forest at dusk.

- **Rose Petals (Rosa spp.)**: Symbolizing love and compassion, these petals are collected from the wild roses that dot the Appalachian landscape, adding a touch of gentle warmth to the blend.

- **Makko Powder**: A natural binder that ensures the incense cones burn consistently, honoring the ancient art of incense making.

- **A Mixing Bowl and Spoon**: For blending the botanicals and makko powder into a harmonious mixture.

- **Distilled Water**: To moisten the blend, facilitating the shaping of the cones and symbolizing the soothing waters of the Appalachian streams.

Preparation: Choose a serene spot where the evening's tranquility can envelop you, perhaps a garden bench or a quiet corner of your porch, where you can witness the sun's final bow. Arrange your materials, letting the peace of the impending night infuse them with stillness.

Crafting the Blend:

1. **Evening Harmony**: Begin with the cedar powder in your mixing bowl, inviting in the essence of stability and protection. Add the juniper berries for their purifying properties, followed by the rose petals to weave in threads of compassion and love.

2. **Unity with Makko**: Introduce the makko powder to your botanicals, ensuring your incense cones will burn smoothly and evenly. The makko serves not just as a binder but as a sacred link to the traditions of incense crafting.

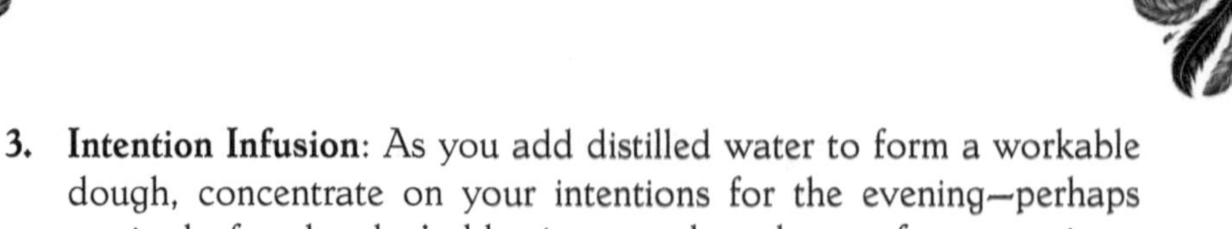

3. **Intention Infusion**: As you add distilled water to form a workable dough, concentrate on your intentions for the evening—perhaps gratitude for the day's blessings or the release of any tensions. With each fold and stir, envision your incense cones radiating calm and grounding energies.

4. **Shaping the Nightfall**: Pinch off small amounts of the dough and shape them into cones, infusing each with your desires for a peaceful evening and a restful night. Place the cones on wax paper to dry, arranging them so they resemble a miniature forest basking in the sunset's glow.

Drying and Charging: Allow the incense cones to dry in a place where the evening air can gently caress them, but shielded from dew and direct moonlight. As they harden, imagine them absorbing the serene energy of the Appalachian twilight, becoming vessels of peace and reflection.

Evening Invocation: With each sunset during the drying process, affirm your intentions with a simple chant or prayer, such as, "As the sun sets on this day, I infuse these cones with the calm of the twilight, the protection of cedar, the purification of juniper, and the love of the rose. May they bring peace to my heart and home."

Closing the Ritual: Once fully dried, gather your incense cones, offering thanks to the evening sky, the land, and the botanicals that have lent their energies to your creation. Store them in a place where they can remain undisturbed until you are ready to use them, each cone a reminder of the tranquility and beauty of Appalachian sunsets.

This ritual, rooted in the essence of the Appalachian evenings, allows you to carry the peace of twilight into your home and heart. The incense cones crafted through this sacred process serve as beacons of calm, guiding you through the night with the gentle, loving embrace of the dusk.

Preserving and Storing Incense

The art of crafting incense is an ancient and sacred practice, deeply embedded in the Appalachian tradition of smoke magic. Each blend, stick, or cone you create carries not only the aromatic essence of the natural world but also the intentions and energies infused during its making. To maintain the potency and integrity of these creations, proper preservation and storage are paramount. This subsection delves into the best practices for preserving your homemade incense, offering practical advice to ensure that each use is as meaningful and potent as the first.

Preservation Techniques: Guarding the Essence

The preservation of incense is crucial to maintaining its fragrance and efficacy in ritual and magical work. The key factors in preserving incense include protecting it from sunlight, moisture, and air exposure.

- **Airtight Containers**: The most effective way to preserve incense is by storing it in airtight containers. Oxygen can degrade the aromatic compounds over time, while airtight conditions help retain the incense's natural fragrance and potency.

- **Sunlight and Moisture**: Direct sunlight can cause the essential oils in incense to evaporate, diminishing its aroma and potency. Similarly, moisture can lead to mold growth, especially in more humid climates. Store your incense in a cool, dark place to protect it from these elements.

- **Aging Incense**: Much like fine wine, certain incense blends can improve with age. The aging process allows the ingredients to meld together more cohesively, often enhancing the overall aroma and potency. Consider setting aside some incense blends in a dedicated aging container, noting the start date of the aging process.

Storage Solutions: Sanctuaries for Sacred Scents

The containers and spaces we choose to store our incense can contribute to its preservation and the maintenance of its magical integrity.

- **Natural Materials**: Opt for storage containers made from natural materials like glass, wood, or cotton. Glass jars with tight-sealing lids are ideal for loose incense blends, while wooden boxes can

offer a breathable yet protected environment for incense sticks and cones. Cotton pouches imbued with herbs like lavender or rosemary can add an additional layer of aromatic and protective energy.

- **Consecration and Blessing**: To enhance the protective qualities of your storage solutions, consider consecrating or blessing them. This can be done through a simple ritual involving smudging the container with sage, cedar, or another purifying incense, and imbuing it with your intention for protection and preservation. A verbal blessing or the placement of a protective sigil on the container can also reinforce its role as a guardian of your incense.

Labeling and Organization: The Art of Order

A well-organized and labeled incense collection is not only practical but also enhances the ritual experience, allowing you to select the perfect blend with ease and intention.

- **Labeling**: Each incense blend, stick, or cone should be labeled with its name, ingredients, date of creation, and intended purpose or magical properties. This practice not only aids in organization but also serves as a record of your incense crafting journey, allowing you to replicate or tweak recipes in the future.

- **Organizational Tips**: Organize your incense collection in a way that resonates with your practice and space. You might categorize incense by its purpose (e.g., purification, protection, healing), by season, or by the primary botanical used. Consider creating a dedicated incense cabinet or shelf, where each blend is displayed and easily accessible, turning your collection into both a functional and aesthetic element of your sacred space.

In preserving and storing your incense, you honor the time, effort, and intention that went into its creation. These practices not only ensure the longevity of your incense but also deepen your connection to the craft, embedding a sense of sacredness and reverence in every aspect of your smoke magic practice. By treating each blend, stick, and cone as a cherished ally in your magical workings, you create a harmonious flow between the act of crafting and the act of ritual, each enhancing the other in a continuous cycle of creation and transformation.

Concluding Thoughts

As we draw the curtains on Chapter 5, "Crafting Your Incense," we stand at the threshold of a deeper understanding and appreciation of the ancient art of incense-making within the rich tapestry of Appalachian traditions. This chapter has been a journey through the fragrant forests and mist-covered hills of Appalachia, guiding us in harnessing the natural abundance of this sacred land to create incense that is not only aromatic but deeply imbued with intention and purpose.

Through the detailed step-by-step guides, we've learned how to transform the humble offerings of sage, cedar, pine, and lavender—each a whisper of the Appalachian wilds—into potent blends, sticks, and cones. We've delved into the alchemy of combining these botanicals, guided by our intentions, whether for purification, protection, healing, or communion with the spirit realm. This process of creation is a sacred dialogue, a dance of elements, and a celebration of the interconnectedness of all life.

The act of formulating intentions and carefully selecting corresponding materials has reminded us that incense-making is more than a craft; it is a magical practice, a way of weaving our desires and prayers into the very fabric of the material world. Each herb, each resin, each wood has been a teacher, imparting lessons of resilience, healing, and protection, and inviting us to listen more deeply to the whispers of the earth.

Preserving and storing our incense with reverence ensures that the energy and effort invested in its creation are honored, safeguarding the potency and integrity of our magical allies. This practice of preservation is a reflection of our respect for the materials we use and our commitment to walking lightly upon the earth, taking only what we need and giving back in gratitude.

As we close this chapter, we are reminded that each incense blend we craft is a reflection of our unique connection to the Appalachian landscape and its spirit. The act of burning our incense becomes a sacred ritual, a way of returning the gifts of the land to the heavens in spirals of fragrant smoke, bridging the earthly and the divine.

"Crafting Your Incense" has not only equipped us with the practical skills to create our incense but has also deepened our relationship with the natural world and the ancient traditions of Appalachia. As we continue our journey through "Sacred Smoke and Mountain Spirits," let us carry forward the spirit of reverence, intention, and harmony that infuses every aspect of Appalachian incense-making, allowing it to illuminate our path and enrich our practice of smoke magic.

Chapter 6:
The Art of Smudging

TRADITIONAL APPALACHIAN SMUDGING RITUALS AND TECHNIQUES

Within the Appalachian tradition, the sacred act of smudging is a deeply revered practice, rooted in the rich confluence of cultural heritages that make up the tapestry of this region. This ancient ritual, blending the wisdom of Indigenous, European, African, and other lineages, serves as a powerful means of purification, protection, and spiritual communication. As we explore the art of smudging in the Appalachian context, we uncover a practice that is both a homage to the past and a living tradition that continues to evolve and enrich the spiritual lives of those who walk these ancient lands.

Historical Context: The Roots of Appalachian Smudging

The practice of smudging in Appalachia is a vibrant mosaic, shaped by the diverse cultures that have found a home in these mountains. Indigenous peoples, with their deep understanding of the land and its spirits, have long used the smoke of sacred herbs to cleanse, bless, and heal. European settlers brought with them the traditions of burning aromatic plants for protection and ceremonial purposes. Enslaved Africans, despite being forcibly brought to these shores, preserved their ancestral knowledge of smoke rituals for cleansing and spiritual protection. Together, these threads weave a rich tapestry of smudging practices that reflect the resilience, adaptability, and spiritual depth of the Appalachian people.

Rituals Overview: Purification, Protection, and Communion

Smudging rituals in Appalachia are as varied as the people who practice them, yet they share common purposes that resonate with the universal human experience.

- **Purification**: One of the most common uses of smudging is to purify a person, object, or space of negative energies, emotions, or spirits. This is often done in preparation for sacred ceremonies, to cleanse a new home, or to clear one's aura after a challenging experience.

- **Protection**: Smudging with specific herbs like sage, cedar, or sweetgrass creates a protective barrier against negative influences. This

practice is particularly sought after during times of vulnerability, such as during healing processes or significant life transitions.

◆ **Communication with the Spiritual Realm**: Smudging can also serve as a medium for connecting with ancestors, spirits, and deities. The rising smoke is believed to carry prayers and intentions to the spiritual realm, facilitating a dialogue between the worlds.

◆ **Seasonal and Life Transitions**: In Appalachia, smudging is often intertwined with the marking of seasonal changes, such as solstices and equinoxes, and significant life events like births, marriages, and passings. These rituals acknowledge the cyclical nature of life and the ever-present connection between the physical and spiritual realms.

Techniques and Tools: The Hows and Whys of Appalachian Smudging

The techniques employed in Appalachian smudging rituals are as important as the intentions behind them. Each movement, each tool, carries its own symbolism and purpose.

◆ **Wafting Smoke**: The act of gently wafting smoke towards oneself or around a space is central to smudging. This can be done with the hands, but often, feathers or fans are used to direct the smoke more precisely. Feathers, especially those from birds like the eagle or owl, are believed to carry the added protection and wisdom of these sacred creatures.

◆ **Significance of Directions**: Many smudging rituals involve moving in specific directions, often starting from the east, the direction of new beginnings and moving clockwise. This movement honors the natural flow of energy and the cycle of the sun across the sky.

◆ **Traditional Tools**: In addition to smudge sticks made from bundled herbs, traditional Appalachian smudging might include the use of shells or clay pots to hold the burning herbs, symbolizing the element of water or earth, respectively. These vessels are often passed down through generations, carrying the ancestral blessings and energies with them.

In the Appalachian tradition, smudging is more than a ritual; it is a way of life, a means of maintaining harmony and balance with the natural and spiritual worlds. As we delve deeper into the nuances of this sacred practice, we not only honor the wisdom of those who have come before us but also contribute to the living tradition that continues to flourish in the heart of Appalachia.

CREATING SMUDGE STICKS FROM APPALACHIAN HERBS AND PLANTS

In the heart of Appalachia, where the air is filled with the whispers of ancient forests and the wisdom of the mountains, the tradition of crafting smudge sticks from the land's bountiful herbs and plants is a sacred art. This practice, deeply rooted in the spiritual heritage of the region, harnesses the cleansing and purifying energies of native flora to create powerful tools for smudging rituals. This section will guide you through the selection of herbs, their ethical harvesting and preparation, and the spiritual process of blessing the smudge sticks, ensuring that each one carries the profound energies of the Appalachian landscape.

Herb Selection: The Foundation of Appalachian Smudging

The choice of herbs and plants for smudging sticks is pivotal, each botanical bringing its unique energies and properties to the smudging ritual.

- **White Sage (Salvia apiana)**: Revered for its strong cleansing properties, white sage is often used to purify spaces, objects, and individuals, clearing away negative energies and offering protection.

- **Sweetgrass (Hierochloe odorata)**: Known for its sweet, uplifting aroma, sweetgrass is used to invite positive energies, peace, and harmony, often after sage has cleared negative influences.

- **Cedar (Juniperus virginiana)**: Cedar's robust and protective energies make it a staple in smudging practices, used for purification and to create a safe, sacred space.

- **Tobacco (Nicotiana tabacum)**: Tobacco is a sacred plant in many Indigenous traditions, used in offerings and prayers for its ability to carry messages to the spirit world.

Harvesting and Preparation: Respectful Gathering and Care

The harvesting of these sacred plants is an act of deep respect and connection to the Earth, guided by principles of sustainability and gratitude.

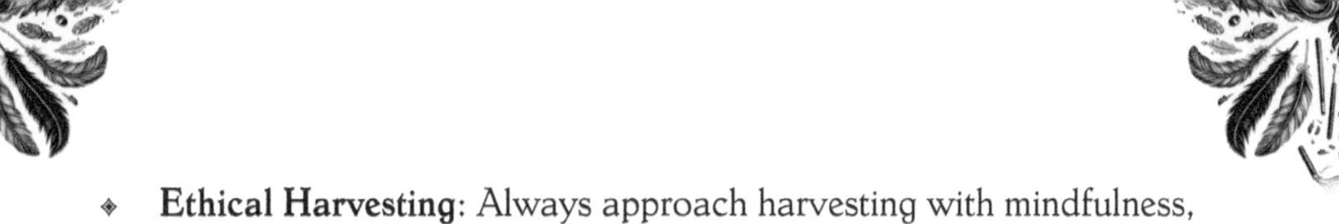

- **Ethical Harvesting**: Always approach harvesting with mindfulness, taking only what you need and leaving enough for the plant to continue thriving. It's important to give thanks to the plant and, if possible, offer something in return, such as water or a small stone, as a gesture of gratitude and reciprocity.

- **Preparation**: Once harvested, the plants should be carefully cleaned and allowed to dry. This can be done by tying them in small bundles and hanging them upside down in a dry, well-ventilated area away from direct sunlight. The drying process can take several days to a few weeks, depending on the plant and the humidity levels.

- **Bundling**: To create smudge sticks, select a mixture of dried herbs that align with your intended purpose. Lay them out on a clean cloth, arranging them into a bundle. Begin at the base, wrapping the bundle tightly with a natural thread, such as cotton or hemp, moving upward in a spiral pattern. Secure the top with a knot, then trim any excess thread and herbs to create a neat, uniform stick.

Blessing the Smudge Sticks: Infusing with Intent and Spirit

The final step in the creation of smudge sticks is their blessing—a ritual act that imbues the sticks with specific energies and intentions.

- **Ritual Cleansing**: Before blessing the smudge sticks, cleanse the space and yourself using a previously made smudge stick or other cleansing methods. This purifies the environment and sets a sacred tone for the blessing process.

- **Setting Intentions**: Hold the smudge stick in your hands, closing your eyes and focusing on your intentions. Whether it's for protection, healing, purification, or communication with the spirit realm, clearly visualize your goal and the energy you wish to imbue the stick with.

- **Blessing Prayer or Chant**: With your intentions set, recite a prayer, chant, or affirmation that encapsulates the purpose of the smudge stick. For example, "May this smudge stick carry the cleansing energy of sage, the harmony of sweetgrass, the protection of cedar, and the sacred breath of tobacco. May it purify and protect the spaces it touches and carry our prayers to the spirits."

- **Concluding the Ritual**: To conclude, pass the smudge stick through the smoke of another burning smudge stick or over a candle flame to symbolically seal the blessing. Give thanks to the plants, the

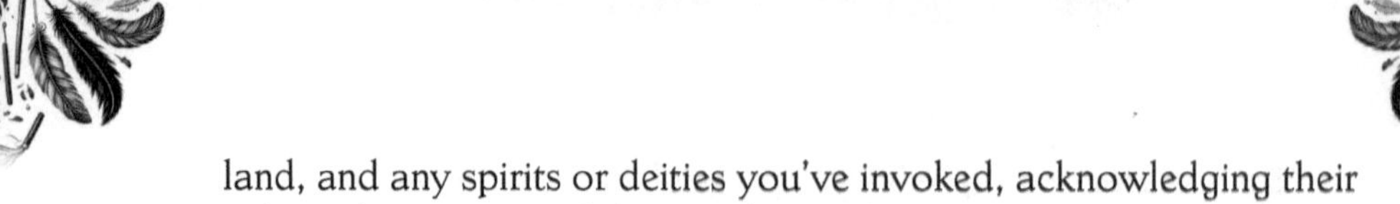

land, and any spirits or deities you've invoked, acknowledging their role in the creation of the smudge stick.

Crafting smudge sticks from Appalachian herbs and plants is a practice that connects us to the rhythms of the earth and the ancient traditions of the land. Each step, from the careful selection and harvesting of herbs to the mindful blessing of the finished sticks, is a testament to the sacredness of this practice. These smudge sticks, imbued with the energies of the Appalachian wilds, become powerful allies in our spiritual journeys, guiding us towards balance, purity, and a deeper connection to the natural world.

GUIDELINES FOR SMUDGING SPACES, OBJECTS, AND INDIVIDUALS

Smudging, an ancient practice rooted deeply in Appalachian and various indigenous traditions, serves as a powerful tool for cleansing and sanctifying spaces, objects, and individuals. This sacred act, when performed with intention and respect, can facilitate profound transformations, ushering in purified energies and fostering environments conducive to healing, growth, and spiritual connection. This section delves into the nuanced practices of smudging, offering detailed guidance to ensure these rituals are conducted with depth, reverence, and effectiveness.

Smudging Spaces: Sanctifying the Sacred and the Everyday

The smudging of spaces, whether they be homes, workplaces, or areas designated for spiritual practice, is a fundamental aspect of maintaining energetic hygiene and harmony. The process involves not only the physical act of smudging but also a deep engagement with the space through intention and presence.

1. **Preparation and Intention**: Begin by ventilating the area, opening windows and doors to allow the passage of smoke and the energies it carries. Center yourself, grounding in the purpose of your smudging ritual, whether it's cleansing after a conflict, blessing a new home, or preparing for a sacred ceremony.

2. **Commencing the Ritual**: Light your smudge stick, allowing it to smolder and produce smoke. Start at the entrance of the space, acknowledging it as the threshold between the external world and the sanctified interior.

3. **Mindful Coverage**: Proceed through the space methodically, guiding the smoke into all corners, along walls, around doorways, and through windows. These areas often accumulate stagnant energies and should be given special attention to ensure a comprehensive cleansing.

4. **Affirmation and Sealing**: As you move through the space, vocalize your intentions, using affirmations, prayers, or chants that resonate

with the purpose of your smudging. Conclude the ritual by returning to the entrance, sealing the purified energy within the space and expressing gratitude for the renewal.

Smudging Objects: Cleansing the Material Extensions of Our World

Objects, from the tools used in our daily rituals to the treasures that hold sentimental value, carry energies that can be cleansed and revitalized through smudging.

1. **Selection and Intention**: Choose the objects to be smudged, whether they are new acquisitions requiring energetic alignment, tools of your craft seeking purification, or personal items needing rejuvenation.

2. **The Act of Cleansing**: Ignite the smudge stick, and carefully pass each object through the smoke, enveloping it completely. This act is not merely about the physical contact with smoke but about the object's reconnection with the natural world and the cleansing of energies it has absorbed.

3. **Blessing and Energizing**: As you smudge each object, imbue it with your intentions—be it protection, clarity, or love. Visualize the smoke as a conduit for these energies, transforming the object into a vibrantly aligned tool or talisman.

Smudging Individuals: A Sacred Exchange of Energy and Intention

Smudging individuals is a practice steeped in trust, respect, and the shared acknowledgment of the sacredness inherent in each of us. Whether smudging oneself as an act of self-care or another as a gesture of healing, the process is delicate and profound.

1. **Consent and Comfort**: Always seek explicit consent before smudging another individual, ensuring they are comfortable with the process and the intentions behind it. This is a fundamental aspect of respect and personal boundaries within the ritual.

2. **Technique and Flow**: For self-smudging, begin at the feet and move upward in a spiraling motion, allowing the smoke to encircle and uplift. When smudging another, maintain a respectful distance, guiding the smoke around their body with gentle movements, focusing on areas that are energetically significant or requested by the individual.

3. **Setting Intentions**: Whether for purification, protection, or blessing, clearly articulate the intentions behind the smudging. Encourage the individual being smudged to focus on their breath, visualizing the smoke carrying away any energies that no longer serve them, leaving room for light and renewal.

4. **Closing and Gratitude**: Conclude the smudging with words of thanks—to the plants that provided the smudge, to the spirits or energies invoked during the ritual, and to the individual for their openness to the process. This closure marks a return to the ordinary flow of life, now enriched by the sacred act of smudging.

Through these guidelines for smudging spaces, objects, and individuals, we tap into an ancient wellspring of wisdom and connection. Each act of smudging is a thread in the larger tapestry of our lives, interwoven with the energies of the earth, the community, and the self. Performed with intention and respect, smudging becomes a transformative practice, aligning our environments, possessions, and personal energies with the highest good and fostering spaces of peace, clarity, and spiritual nourishment.

APPALACHIAN HEARTH AND HOME SMUDGING RITUAL WITH BINDING INSTRUCTIONS

In the tranquil moments of dawn, as the Appalachian landscape stirs to life under a canopy of mist and the soft hues of the sunrise, a time-honored ritual begins. The Appalachian Hearth and Home Smudging Ritual is a deeply rooted practice, dedicated to cleansing, protecting, and harmonizing the home. Drawing from the rich bounty of the mountains, this ritual combines the sacred energies of indigenous herbs to create a protective and nurturing atmosphere within the domestic sphere.

Materials Needed:

- **White Sage (Salvia apiana) Bundle**: Emblematic of purification, this sage is gathered with respect from the Appalachian wilds.

- **Cedar (Juniperus virginiana) Branches**: Symbolizing strength and protection, cedar branches reflect the enduring nature of the mountains.

- **Sweetgrass (Hierochloe odorata) Braid**: Representing peace, harmony, and the goodwill of the ancestors.

- ◆ **A Feather or Fan**: For directing the sacred smoke, embodying the element of air and the whispers of the spirit.

- ◆ **A Fireproof Bowl or Shell**: To safely hold the burning herbs, symbolizing the nurturing cradle of the earth.

Preparation: Choose a serene time for the ritual, ideally at dawn when the home is quiet, and the day is beginning. Open windows and doors to allow the flow of fresh mountain air, preparing the space for the cleansing ritual.

Binding the Smudge Stick:

1. **Laying the Foundations**: Spread out a clean cloth and place your white sage at the center. This sage will form the core of your smudge stick, intended for purification.

2. **Adding Cedar**: Lay thin branches of cedar atop the sage. The cedar acts as a protective layer, enveloping the sage with its strength.

3. **Weaving in Sweetgrass**: Intertwine strands of sweetgrass around the sage and cedar, infusing the bundle with harmony and positive energy.

4. **Securing the Bundle**: Using a natural twine or cotton string, start at the base of your herb bundle. Hold the end of the string with your thumb and begin wrapping tightly upward, ensuring each layer overlaps slightly to hold the herbs in place.

5. **Final Knot**: Once you reach the top of the bundle, loop the string around several times before bringing it back down in a crisscross pattern. Secure the string with a firm knot at the base where you started. Trim any excess string and straighten out the herbs for a neat finish.

The Ritual:

1. **Ignition of Intent**: Light the smudge stick, allowing it to flame briefly before blowing it out, letting it smolder and smoke. Place it in your fireproof container.

2. **Threshold Blessing**: Begin at your front door, using the feather or fan to spread smoke around the frame, setting a protective boundary while stating, "By sage, cedar, and sweetgrass, this door is shielded, allowing only light and love to enter."

3. **Hearth Purification**: Move to the heart of your home, smudging around the central living area or kitchen, focusing on cleansing and unity, saying, "Let this hearth glow with warmth, harmony, and joy, a sanctuary for all."

4. **Room-by-Room Cleansing**: Continue through each room, particularly targeting corners and hidden spaces, envisioning the dispelling of all negative energy and the ushering in of peace and clarity.

5. **Sweetgrass Seal**: Conclude by threading sweetgrass through the central areas, inviting an influx of positive energy and blessings with, "Sweetgrass weaves harmony and blessings into this home, embraced by the spirit of peace."

Closing the Ritual: With the completion of the smudging, feel the renewed energy within your home. Express gratitude to the sage, cedar, and sweetgrass, to the Appalachian lands, and to any guiding spirits. Extinguish the smudge stick safely, preserving it for future rituals.

This ritual, grounded in Appalachian tradition, transforms your home into a bastion of tranquility and protection. Through the deliberate act of binding the herbs, you weave together the protective forces of nature, creating a smudge stick that is not only a tool but a sacred talisman for your home.

APPALACHIAN ARTIFACT RENEWAL SMUDGING RITUAL

In the stillness of the Appalachian twilight, as the day melds into the night and the air is filled with the gentle chorus of the forest, a sacred ritual unfolds to cleanse and consecrate cherished objects. The Appalachian Artifact Renewal Smudging Ritual is a venerable practice, rooted in the deep spiritual connection to the land and its gifts, designed to imbue objects with the protective, purifying, and harmonizing energies of the mountains.

Materials Needed:

1. **Mountain Mint (Pycnanthemum virginianum) Bundle**: Gathered from the heart of Appalachia, mountain mint is known for its refreshing and protective properties, perfect for revitalizing objects with its crisp, cleansing energy.

2. **Dogwood (Cornus florida) Twigs**: Symbolizing durability and re-silience, dogwood twigs add a layer of strength and endurance to the smudging ritual.

3. **Blackberry Leaves (Rubus spp.)**: Representing abundance and protection, blackberry leaves are woven into the ritual to shield and nurture the object's inherent energies.

4. **A Feather or Fan**: To gracefully direct the sacred smoke, symboliz-ing the breath of the mountains and the whispers of the ancestors.

5. **A Fireproof Bowl or Shell**: Cradling the embers of the smudge stick, this vessel embodies the earth's grounding and supportive energy.

Preparation: Select a tranquil moment for the ritual, preferably as dusk falls, when the world transitions from daylight to darkness, re-flecting the renewal process. Arrange the space where the object will be cleansed, inviting the evening's calm to permeate the surroundings.

Binding the Smudge Stick:

1. **Foundation of Cleansing**: On a clean surface, lay out the mountain mint, setting the stage for a thorough purification of the object.

2. **Layer of Resilience**: Place dogwood twigs atop the mint, channel-ing the enduring spirit of the Appalachian woodlands.

3. **Leaves of Protection**: Intersperse blackberry leaves within the bun-dle, ensuring the object is encased in a protective embrace.

4. **Binding for Renewal**: Secure the herbs and twigs together with a natural cord, winding tightly from base to top, each wrap symbol-izing a layer of cleansing, protection, and strength.

5. **Sealing the Energy**: Upon reaching the bundle's top, wrap the cord multiple times before descending in a diagonal pattern to the base. Knot the cord securely, infusing the final tie with your intention for the ritual.

The Ritual:

1. **Ignition of Purification**: Light the smudge stick, allowing it to brief-ly ignite before blowing it out, leaving a smoldering ember that releases a purifying smoke. Nestle it in your fireproof container.

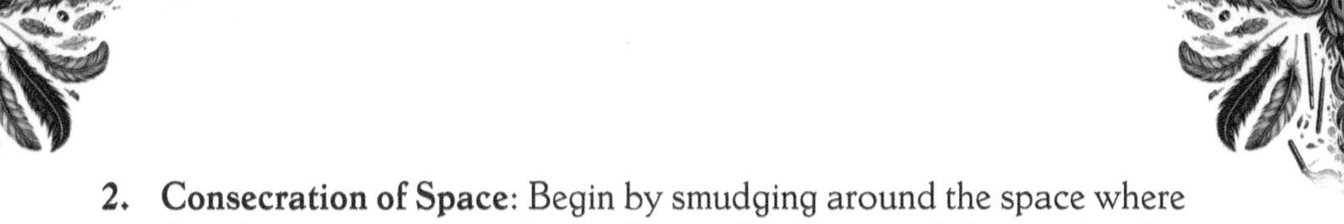

2. **Consecration of Space**: Begin by smudging around the space where the object rests, using the feather or fan to spread the smoke, declaring, "With mountain mint, dogwood, and blackberry, I sanctify this space, welcoming in the cleansing breath of the mountains."

3. **Object Purification**: Carefully waft the smoke over and around the object, envisioning any lingering energies being dissolved and carried away by the smoke. "Through this smoke, I release all that no longer serves, cleansing and renewing this object to its original purity and purpose."

4. **Infusion of Intent**: Hold the object within the smoke, focusing on your intentions for it—whether for protection, healing, or spiritual connection. "May this object be reborn through the sacred smoke, imbued with the resilience of dogwood, the abundance of blackberry, and the protective embrace of the mint."

5. **Blessing of Renewal**: Conclude the ritual by encircling the object with smoke once more, sealing in the new energies and blessings. "Encased in the spirit of the mountains, this object stands renewed, a beacon of light and protector in my journey."

Closing the Ritual: As the twilight deepens, acknowledge the completion of the cleansing, expressing gratitude to the herbs, the land, and the guiding spirits. Carefully extinguish the smudge stick, preserving it for future use.

This ritual, steeped in the traditions of Appalachian spirituality, transforms objects into sacred talismans, each carrying the essence of the mountains and the protective, renewing energies of the native herbs. Through the mindful binding of the smudge stick and the intentional smudging process, cherished artifacts are reborn, ready to serve their purpose with renewed vigor and sanctity.

APPALACHIAN PERSONAL RENEWAL SMUDGING RITUAL

In the serene embrace of an Appalachian morning, where the dew glistens on the underbrush and the air is fresh with the scent of pine and earth, a deeply personal ritual unfolds. The Appalachian Personal Renewal Smudging Ritual is a practice of self-purification and spiritual rejuvenation, drawing upon the ancient wisdom and natural bounty of the mountains to cleanse the aura and refresh the spirit.

Materials Needed:

- **Witch Hazel (Hamamelis virginiana) Leaves**: Collected from the heart of the forest, witch hazel is known for its healing and protective properties, making it ideal for personal cleansing.

- **Black Cohosh (Actaea racemosa) Roots**: Revered for its grounding and strength-building qualities, black cohosh roots add depth and resilience to the smudging ritual.

- **Mullein (Verbascum thapsus) Flowers and Leaves**: Symbolizing clarity and cleansing, mullein aids in the purification of the respiratory system and the energetic field.

- **A Feather or Fan**: To softly distribute the sacred smoke, embodying the gentle caress of the mountain breeze and the guiding hand of the ancestors.

- **A Fireproof Bowl or Shell**: Safeguarding the embers of the smudge stick, this vessel represents the earth's stability and support.

Preparation: Select a quiet, reflective moment for the ritual, ideally in the early hours when the world is awakening. Find a peaceful spot where you can stand barefoot on the earth, connecting directly with the land's grounding energy.

Binding the Smudge Stick:

1. **Foundation of Healing**: Arrange witch hazel leaves on a clean surface, laying the groundwork for protection and healing.

2. **Roots of Strength**: Place pieces of black cohosh root among the witch hazel, infusing the bundle with deep, earthy resilience.

3. **Cleansing Blooms and Leaves**: Add mullein flowers and leaves to the mix, enhancing the smudge stick with their purifying essence.

4. **Binding for Renewal**: Carefully wrap the herbs and roots with a natural fiber, securing them tightly from the bottom up, each layer symbolizing a step towards personal purification and renewal.

5. **Knot of Intent**: Once at the top, secure the bundle with multiple loops before winding back down in a diagonal pattern. Tie off the string with a firm knot at the base, imbuing it with your intentions for the ritual.

The Ritual:

1. **Ignition of Self-Purification**: Light the smudge stick, letting it burn briefly before blowing it out to produce a gentle stream of smoke. Hold it within your fireproof container.

2. **Aura Cleansing**: Begin by circling the smudge stick around your body, starting at your feet and moving upward in a spiral motion. Use the feather or fan to guide the smoke around your form, focusing on areas of tension or heaviness.

3. **Intentional Breathing**: With each pass of the smoke, take deep, intentional breaths, visualizing the smoke carrying away any negativity, stress, or stagnant energy from your aura.

4. **Centering and Grounding**: Bring the smudge stick to your heart center, allowing the smoke to envelop you. Affirm your connection to the earth and the mountains, stating, "With witch hazel, black cohosh, and mullein, I cleanse my spirit, ground my being, and renew my connection to the land and my purpose."

5. **Sealing the Ritual**: Conclude by drawing the smoke over your head, envisioning a crown of clarity and protection. Express gratitude to the plants, the land, and any guiding spirits or ancestors for their support in your renewal.

Closing the Ritual: As the smoke dissipates, feel the lightness and clarity within your being. Take a moment to reflect on the renewed sense of connection to yourself and the natural world. Safely extinguish the smudge stick, reserving it for future moments of personal cleansing and reflection.

This ritual, rooted in the traditions and natural splendor of Appalachia, transforms the act of smudging into a deeply personal journey of purification and rebirth. Through the mindful selection and binding of native herbs, and the intentional practice of self-smudging, you reaffirm your place within the cycle of life and the eternal flow of renewal that defines the Appalachian spirit.

Concluding Thoughts

As we draw the final strokes on Chapter 6, "The Art of Smudging," we find ourselves enveloped in the fragrant embrace of smoke, carrying the deep wisdom and spiritual resonance of the Appalachian traditions. This chapter has been a journey through the sacred practice of smudging, a path that weaves through the living tapestry of the mountains, forests, and streams that define the Appalachian landscape.

In exploring the traditional Appalachian smudging rituals and techniques, we've delved into the heart of a practice that transcends mere cleansing, becoming a profound means of communication between the physical and spiritual realms. We've learned that smudging is not just an act of purification but a ritual of reconnection, a way to honor the past, sanctify the present, and bless the future.

The creation of smudge sticks from the rich bounty of Appalachian herbs and plants has connected us more deeply to the land, reminding us of the intricate relationships that sustain life. Each plant carries a story, a spirit, and an energy that contributes to the sacred act of smudging, allowing us to harness their unique gifts for protection, healing, and harmony.

Guidelines for smudging spaces, objects, and individuals have provided us with practical tools to integrate this ancient practice into our daily lives, offering ways to cleanse our homes, sanctify our tools, and purify our auras. These rituals bring the ancient wisdom of the Appalachians into our modern lives, allowing us to create sanctuaries of peace, centers of clarity, and vessels of sacred energy.

As we conclude this chapter, we carry forward the knowledge that smudging is more than a ritual—it is a way of life. It is a practice that calls us to live in harmony with the natural world, to honor the spirits that dwell in the land, and to recognize the sacredness in all beings and objects. In embracing the art of smudging, we open ourselves to the transformative power of smoke, allowing it to cleanse, bless, and renew not just our physical spaces but our hearts and spirits as well.

"Sacred Smoke and Mountain Spirits" has invited us to walk in the footsteps of the ancestors, to learn from the plants and the spirits of

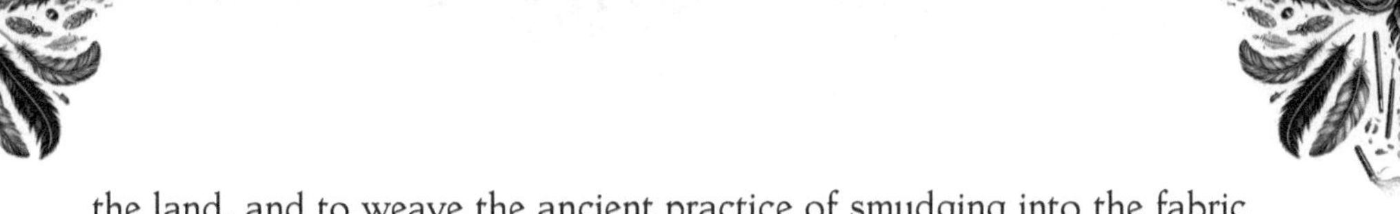

the land, and to weave the ancient practice of smudging into the fabric of our lives. As we move forward, let us do so with reverence for the traditions that have been passed down to us, with gratitude for the gifts of the earth, and with a commitment to carrying the sacred flame of Appalachian smudging into the future.

Chapter 7:
Incense for the Seasons

Seasonal Incense Recipes and Smudging Rituals That Align with the Appalachian Wheel of the Year

The Appalachian Wheel of the Year spins through cycles of birth, growth, harvest, and rest, each turn marked by the changing seasons and their corresponding celebrations. This rhythm, deeply ingrained in the land and its inhabitants, offers a rich tapestry for integrating the practice of incense making and smudging into the seasonal flow of life. This section delves into the crafting of seasonal incense blends and the rituals that accompany the Wheel of the Year, inviting us to attune our practices to the natural cycle of the Appalachian landscape.

Overview of the Appalachian Wheel of the Year

In the heart of Appalachia, the Wheel of the Year turns in harmony with the cycles of nature, each season offering its unique gifts and challenges. The Wheel begins in the quiet of winter, moves through the awakening of spring, revels in the abundance of summer, and reflects in the harvest of autumn, before returning to the stillness of winter once more. Each quarter and cross-quarter day marks a significant point in this cycle, from the deep rest of Yule to the vibrant growth of Beltane, the abundant harvest of Lughnasadh, and the reflective gratitude of Samhain.

Winter: Embracing the Stillness

As the Wheel turns to Yule, the longest night of the year, the landscape is often blanketed in snow, and life slows to a whisper. This time of introspection and rest is reflected in incense blends rich with evergreen scents, such as pine, cedar, and spruce, which remind us of life's endurance through the cold months.

- **Yule Incense Blend**: Combine pine resin, cedarwood shavings, and a pinch of dried mistletoe. This blend is ideal for smudging during the Winter Solstice, cleansing the home to welcome the rebirth of the sun and the slow return of light.

Spring: Awakening the Earth

With Imbolc and Ostara marking the arrival of spring, the earth stirs from its slumber. Buds begin to bloom, and the air is filled with the promise of renewal. Incense blends for spring are light and fresh, incorporating floral notes like lavender and rose, combined with the bright green of freshly crushed leaves.

- **Spring Equinox Incense Blend**: Mix lavender buds, rose petals, and finely crushed new leaves of birch or lemon balm. Use this blend in rituals to celebrate the balance of light and dark at the Equinox and to invite growth and new beginnings into your life.

Summer: Celebrating the Abundance

As the Wheel turns to Beltane and Midsummer, Appalachia bursts into vibrant life. The forests are lush, and the fields are filled with the hum of activity. Summer incense blends capture the essence of this abundance, featuring the heady aromas of blossoming flowers and the lushness of summer herbs.

- **Midsummer Incense Blend**: Blend together the sun-dried petals of marigold and calendula, with hints of sage and mint. Smudge your space with this blend during the Summer Solstice to honor the peak of the sun's power and the lush abundance of the season.

Autumn: Gathering and Giving Thanks

As the days begin to shorten, the Wheel turns to Lughnasadh and Samhain, bringing the harvest season. It's a time for gathering in and giving thanks for the abundance provided by the land. Incense blends become richer and more grounding, incorporating the spicy scents of cinnamon and clove, mixed with the earthiness of harvested herbs.

- **Samhain Incense Blend**: Combine dried apple slices, cinnamon sticks, and mugwort. This blend is perfect for Samhain rituals, marking the end of the harvest and the beginning of the darker half of the year. It's a time to honor ancestors and the cycle of life and death.

Each of these seasonal incense blends and associated smudging rituals invites us to connect more deeply with the rhythms of the Appalachian landscape and the ancient traditions that honor these cycles. By aligning our practices with the Wheel of the Year, we weave our own lives into the broader tapestry of life, death, rebirth, and renewal that defines the Appalachian spirit. These rituals not only cleanse and sanc-

tify our spaces but also remind us of our place within the natural world, encouraging us to live in harmony with the cycles that govern all life.

WINTER SOLSTICE RENEWAL SMUDGING RITUAL

As the winter solstice approaches, marking the longest night and the return of the light, an ancient and serene ritual unfolds in the quietude of the Appalachian dawn. This Winter Solstice Renewal Smudging Ritual draws upon the dormant yet potent energies of the season, employing a sacred blend of evergreen scents to purify the home and heart, welcoming the gradual rebirth of the sun. Drawing from the deep reservoirs of Appalachian tradition, this ritual combines indigenous herbs to weave a protective and nurturing aura, celebrating the stillness and introspective nature of winter.

Materials Needed:

- **Yule Incense Blend**: Craft a special blend for the solstice by combining pine resin for endurance, cedarwood shavings for strength, and a pinch of dried mistletoe for protection and healing. This blend honors the resilience of life during the cold months and the promise of renewal.

- **A Fireproof Bowl or Shell**: Symbolizing the earth's embrace, this vessel will safely contain the smoldering incense, grounding the ritual in the physical realm.

- **A Feather or Fan**: Representing the element of air, use this tool to spread the sacred smoke, directing it with intention and care throughout your space.

- **Charcoal Disc (if using loose incense)**: To burn the Yule Incense Blend effectively, a charcoal disc placed within the fireproof container will serve as a heat source, igniting the aromatic resins and herbs.

Preparation:

Select a peaceful time on the solstice morning, when the first light begins to crest the horizon, symbolizing the return of the sun. Prepare your space by opening windows slightly, allowing the new energies to enter and the old to depart, mirroring the cycle of renewal inherent in the season.

Crafting the Yule Incense Blend:

1. **Laying the Foundations**: On a clean surface, arrange your chosen herbs and resins, focusing on their individual and collective meanings—pine for endurance, cedar for protection, and mistletoe for healing.

2. **Combining the Elements**: Mix the pine resin, cedarwood shavings, and mistletoe, blending them with your hands or a mortar and pestle, infusing the mixture with your intentions for renewal, strength, and protection.

3. **Preparing for Ignition**: If using a charcoal disc, light it now and place it in your fireproof bowl or shell, allowing it to become hot. Once ready, sprinkle your Yule Incense Blend atop the glowing charcoal, inviting the aromatic smoke to rise.

The Ritual:

1. **Ignition of Intent**: As the incense begins to smolder, set your intention for the ritual. This may be a personal wish for renewal, a prayer for the earth's rejuvenation, or a blessing for your loved ones.

2. **Threshold Blessing**: Start at your home's entrance, using the feather or fan to guide the incense smoke around the doorframe, creating a protective gateway that welcomes positive energies and light.

3. **Hearth Purification**: Proceed to the heart of your home, often the hearth or central gathering space. Here, focus on cleansing and warming the core of your living space, inviting the spirit of the sun to infuse the area with light and warmth.

4. **Room-by-Room Renewal**: Continue to each room, paying special attention to corners, windows, and other spaces where energy can stagnate. As you move, envision the smoke carrying away the old, leaving room for new beginnings and the fresh promise of the coming year.

5. **Solstice Seal**: Conclude the ritual in a central space, perhaps where you gather for meals or celebrations. Here, create a final, dense cloud of smoke, sealing in the blessings of the ritual and the renewed energy brought by the returning light.

Closing the Ritual: With the ritual complete and the incense gently fading, take a moment to reflect on the cycle of darkness and light, of

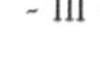

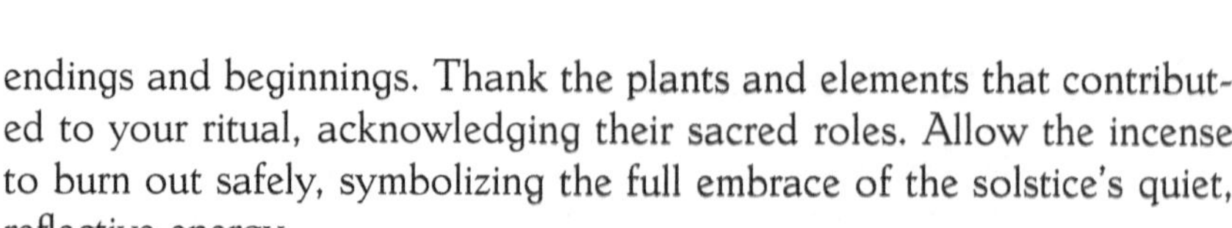

endings and beginnings. Thank the plants and elements that contributed to your ritual, acknowledging their sacred roles. Allow the incense to burn out safely, symbolizing the full embrace of the solstice's quiet, reflective energy.

This Winter Solstice Renewal Smudging Ritual, deeply embedded in the Appalachian tradition, transforms not just the physical spaces of our lives but also our inner landscapes. Through the deliberate crafting of the Yule Incense Blend and the mindful practice of smudging, we honor the depth of winter's stillness and the subtle yet profound return of the light, weaving our intentions and hopes into the fabric of the coming year.

SPRING AWAKENING SMUDGING RITUAL

As the earth transitions from the silent embrace of winter to the vibrant awakening of spring, a harmonious ritual unfolds in the fresh, dew-kissed mornings of Appalachia. The Spring Awakening Smudging Ritual is a celebration of renewal, growth, and the rekindling of life's vibrant energies. Utilizing the tender essences of springtime flora, this ritual is designed to purify and invigorate the home and spirit, aligning with the burgeoning life force of the season.

Materials Needed:

* **Spring Equinox Incense Blend**: Craft an incense blend that encapsulates the essence of spring by mixing fragrant lavender buds, delicate rose petals, and the newly sprouted leaves of birch or lemon balm. This blend honors the burgeoning life, the balance of light and dark, and the fresh beginnings that the Equinox brings.

* **A Feather or Fan**: Representing the gentle yet invigorating breezes of spring, use this tool to guide the cleansing smoke through your space, distributing the season's renewing energies.

* **A Fireproof Bowl or Shell**: This vessel will hold your burning incense safely, grounding your ritual in the stability and nourishment of the earth.

Preparation: Embrace the dawn of a spring morning for this ritual, when the first light filters through the awakening landscape. Prepare your home by opening windows and doors, inviting the fresh, crisp air to cleanse the space and welcome the energies of renewal and growth.

Crafting the Spring Equinox Incense Blend:

1. **Harmonizing the Elements**: On a clear surface, blend your chosen springtime botanicals, focusing on their vibrant energies and the renewal they symbolize. Lavender for tranquility and purification, rose for love and harmony, and birch or lemon balm leaves for new beginnings and healing.

2. **Mingling Scents and Intentions**: Gently combine the lavender, rose, and birch or lemon balm, infusing the blend with your intentions for balance, renewal, and growth. Each component contributes its unique qualities to create a harmonious whole.

The Ritual:

1. **Ignition of Renewal**: Light your Spring Equinox Incense Blend, allowing it to smolder and release its fragrant smoke. Place it within your fireproof container as a focal point for the ritual.

2. **Blessing of Beginnings**: Starting at your entrance, use the feather or fan to spread the incense smoke gently around the doorway, inviting the energies of growth and renewal into your home. As you do so, articulate your intentions for the season, such as "With the scents of lavender, rose, and birch, I welcome the renewing energies of spring into this space and my heart."

3. **Core Purification**: Proceed to the central part of your home, the hearth or communal gathering area, and allow the smoke to envelop this space. Here, focus on revitalizing the heart of your home, imbuing it with the vibrancy and potential of the season.

4. **Sweep of Renewal**: Continue through each room, paying special attention to areas that have felt dormant or stagnant. Envision the smoke as a gentle force, awakening and purifying each space, much like the spring sun melts away the last vestiges of winter snow.

5. **Sealing of Spring's Promise**: Conclude your ritual in a place where you feel most at peace within your home. Create a final dense cloud of the fragrant smoke, sealing the blessings of renewal and growth within your space and spirit.

   Closing the Ritual: With the ritual's completion, take a moment to bask in the fresh energy pervading your home. Express your gratitude to the earth for its endless cycles of renewal, to the plants that have lent their energies, and to any higher powers you invoked during the ritual.

Allow the incense to burn out completely, signifying the full embrace of spring's transformative promise.

This Spring Awakening Smudging Ritual, rooted in the rich soil of Appalachian tradition, transforms your home into a sanctuary of renewal, growth, and harmony. Through the deliberate crafting of the Spring Equinox Incense Blend and the mindful practice of smudging, you honor the reawakening of the earth and invite the vibrant energies of spring into every corner of your life.

Summer Solstice Abundance Smudging Ritual

As the Wheel of the Year spirals towards Beltane and Midsummer, the Appalachian landscape awakens in a riot of color and life. This period of exuberant growth and warmth is the perfect backdrop for the Summer Solstice Abundance Smudging Ritual, a celebration of the sun at its zenith and the lush bounty of the earth. Using a vibrant blend of marigold, calendula, sage, and mint, this ritual is designed to infuse your space with the sun's radiant energy and the verdant abundance of the season.

Materials Needed:

- **Midsummer Incense Blend**: Prepare a potent blend for the solstice by combining the sun-dried petals of marigold and calendula, both symbols of the sun and protection, with hints of sage for wisdom and mint for vitality. This blend is crafted to capture the essence of summer's peak and to sanctify the space with the season's abundant blessings.

- **A Feather or Fan**: Utilize this tool to disperse the smoke throughout your space, symbolizing the light and airy qualities of summer and the gentle touch of the season's warm breezes.

- **A Fireproof Bowl or Shell**: This vessel will hold your incense or smudge stick as it burns, anchoring the ritual in the nurturing and fertile energies of the earth.

Preparation: Opt for an early morning ritual to coincide with the dawn of the Summer Solstice, when the first rays of sunlight illuminate the world. Freshen your space by opening windows to the songs of birds and the scents of blooming flora, setting the stage for a ritual that honors the fullness of life.

Crafting the Midsummer Incense Blend:

1. **Blending the Sun's Rays**: On a clean surface, lay out your marigold and calendula petals, basking in their vibrant colors and solar associations. Add sage and mint to the mix, embracing their cleansing and invigorating properties.

2. **Uniting the Elements**: Gently combine the ingredients, mindful of their individual contributions to the blend. Each element—earth in the herbs, air in the scent, fire in the sun's warmth that dried them, and water in the dew they once held—plays a crucial role in this harmonious union.

The Ritual:

1. **Ignition of Joy**: Light your Midsummer Incense Blend, allowing the bright and aromatic smoke to rise. Position it in your fireproof container, setting a focal point for the sun's energizing presence.

2. **Blessing of Light**: Begin at your threshold, using the feather or fan to waft the incense smoke around your doorway. Invite the sun's boundless energy inside with words of welcome, such as, "With marigold, calendula, sage, and mint, I invite the vibrant energy and abundant blessings of the sun into every corner of this space."

3. **Sanctification of the Hearth**: Proceed to your home's core, the heart where family and friends gather. Allow the smoke to fill this area, weaving through the laughter and memories, and imbuing it with the warmth and vitality of the longest day.

4. **Cleansing Each Nook**: Move through each room, paying special attention to spaces that hold the quiet of winter or the shadows of spring. Visualize the smoke as sunlight in physical form, reaching into every corner to invigorate and renew.

5. **Embrace of Abundance**: Conclude your ritual in an open space, perhaps where meals are shared or where light floods in through windows. Create a dense swirl of incense smoke here, a tangible representation of the sun's life-giving power and the lushness of summer's embrace.

   Closing the Ritual: With the smudging complete and the air rich with the scents of summer, pause to soak in the heightened energy of your home. Offer thanks to the sun for its unwavering light, to the earth for its generous bounty, and to the plants for their sacred essences. Let

the incense burn down as a final homage to the day, symbolizing the ongoing cycle of growth and fulfillment.

This Summer Solstice Abundance Smudging Ritual, deeply rooted in the verdant traditions of Appalachia, transforms not just the physical spaces of our lives but our inner realms as well. Through the mindful blending of midsummer herbs and the deliberate act of smudging, we celebrate the peak of the sun's journey and the abundant life it sustains, weaving the vibrant energies of summer into the fabric of our daily existence.

Autumn Harvest Gratitude Smudging Ritual

In the amber light of autumn, as the Wheel of the Year gently rolls towards Lughnasadh and Samhain, the Appalachian landscape is adorned with the richness of the harvest season. This is a time of gathering, reflection, and giving thanks—a period to honor the abundance bestowed by the earth and to acknowledge the cycles of life and death. The Autumn Harvest Gratitude Smudging Ritual is centered around a special Samhain Incense Blend, designed to draw upon the deep, spicy scents of the season, celebrating the culmination of the year's growth and the ancestral ties that bind us.

Materials Needed:

- **Samhain Incense Blend**: Create a sacred blend for this poignant time of year by uniting the aromatic warmth of dried apple slices and cinnamon sticks with the protective essence of mugwort. This blend serves as a bridge between the worlds, honoring the past and embracing the cycle of renewal.

- **A Feather or Fan**: Symbolic of the winds that usher in the cooler days and longer nights, use this tool to distribute the smoky essence of the incense, carrying your prayers and thanks to the spiritual realm.

- **A Fireproof Bowl or Shell**: This will be the hearth for your incense, a grounding element that connects the ritual to the stability and nurturing energy of the earth.

Preparation: Embrace the ritual at a time when the day's first light paints the world in golden hues, reflecting the season's palette. Prepare your space by inviting the crisp autumn air inside, setting a stage that resonates with the energy of harvest and thanksgiving.

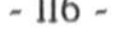

Crafting the Samhain Incense Blend:

1. **Blending the Essence of Autumn**: Arrange the apple slices and cinnamon on a clean surface, their scents mingling with the potent aroma of mugwort. Each ingredient is a testament to the season's character—apples for the harvest, cinnamon for warmth, and mugwort for protection and spiritual connection.

2. **Uniting Scents and Spirits**: Carefully mix these elements, mindful of their roles in the ritual. The act of blending is itself a meditation on the season's themes—abundance, protection, and the thinning veil between worlds.

The Ritual:

1. **Ignition of Reflection**: Light the Samhain Incense Blend, letting it smolder and release its complex fragrance. Place it within your fireproof container as a symbol of the ancestral hearth, a focal point for gathering and giving thanks.

2. **Blessing of Boundaries**: Starting at your home's entrance, use the feather or fan to guide the smoke around the doorway. As you do so, speak words of gratitude for the year's blessings and for the protection and abundance that have been bestowed upon your home, such as, "With the essence of apple, cinnamon, and mugwort, I give thanks for the abundance received and honor the cycle of life and renewal."

3. **Heart of the Home Ceremony**: Move to the central part of your dwelling, where the heart beats strongest with the laughter and love of those who gather there. Let the incense permeate this space, infusing it with the richness of the harvest and the warmth of shared blessings.

4. **Circle of Thanks**: Continue to each room, pausing to acknowledge the year's personal harvests—moments of growth, challenges overcome, and joys celebrated. Envision the smoke as a vehicle for your gratitude, carrying it to every corner of your life.

5. **Ancestral Honor**: Conclude the ritual in a space where you feel connected to your lineage and the cycles of nature. Here, allow the smoke to rise thick and full, a silent prayer to those who have walked the path before you, acknowledging their role in the bounty of the present.

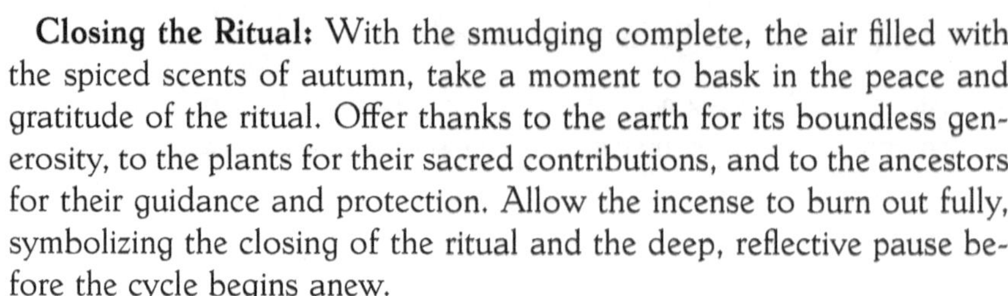

Closing the Ritual: With the smudging complete, the air filled with the spiced scents of autumn, take a moment to bask in the peace and gratitude of the ritual. Offer thanks to the earth for its boundless generosity, to the plants for their sacred contributions, and to the ancestors for their guidance and protection. Allow the incense to burn out fully, symbolizing the closing of the ritual and the deep, reflective pause before the cycle begins anew.

This Autumn Harvest Gratitude Smudging Ritual, woven from the rich tapestry of Appalachian traditions, transforms your space into a sanctuary of thanksgiving and reflection. Through the crafting of the Samhain Incense Blend and the deliberate act of smudging, we connect more deeply with the rhythms of the earth, the legacy of our ancestors, and the cycle of life and death that underscores the human experience, grounding us in the profound beauty of the harvest season.

CELEBRATING SEASONAL FESTIVALS WITH SMOKE MAGIC

The rhythmic cycle of the seasons in Appalachia, with its vibrant festivals and solemn ceremonies, offers a rich tapestry for integrating the ancient art of smoke magic. This tradition, deeply rooted in the land and its people, serves not only to enhance the ambiance of these gatherings but to deepen their spiritual resonance. By incorporating incense and smudging into these time-honored celebrations, we invite a tangible sense of the sacred into our communal and solitary observances, connecting more intimately with the cycles of nature and the energies they embody.

Integrating Incense and Smudging in Festivals

Smoke magic, with its ethereal qualities and profound symbolism, is a powerful tool for marking the passage of the seasons. It serves as a bridge between the tangible and the spiritual, carrying our intentions, blessings, and prayers to the unseen realms. In the context of seasonal festivals, the act of burning incense or smudging with sacred herbs becomes a ritualized expression of the themes inherent in each celebration—renewal and growth in spring, abundance and vitality in summer, gratitude and reflection in autumn, and introspection and renewal in winter.

Spring and Summer Festivities

The lighter half of the year, with its burgeoning life and extended days, brims with opportunities to weave smoke magic into our celebrations:

- **Blessing of the Seeds**: As the earth awakens in spring, rituals to bless the seeds before planting can be enriched with the use of incense crafted from early blooming herbs such as lavender and chamomile. The rising smoke symbolizes the life force awakening in the seeds, carrying our hopes for a bountiful harvest.

- **Purification of Gathering Spaces**: Before summer solstice celebrations or communal gatherings, smudging the area with a blend of sage, sweetgrass, and mint can cleanse the space of lingering nega-

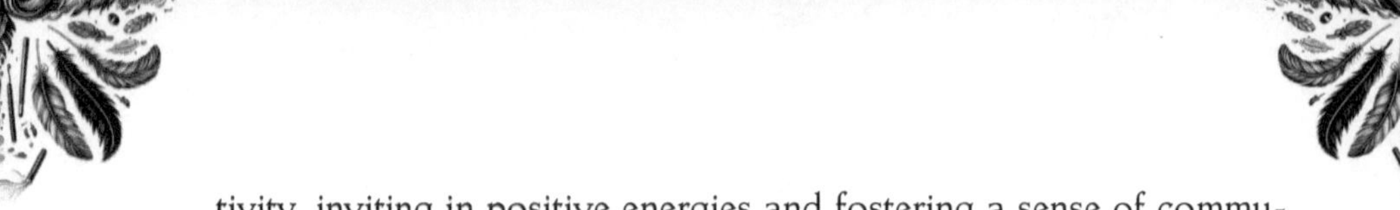

tivity, inviting in positive energies and fostering a sense of communal harmony and joy.

◆ **Midsummer Night's Fires**: The tradition of lighting bonfires during the summer solstice can be complemented by the burning of aromatic herbs like rosemary and thyme, their scents mingling with the fire's smoke to create an atmosphere of protection, purification, and celebration.

Autumn and Winter Ceremonies

As the wheel turns to the darker half of the year, smoke magic becomes a vessel for deeper introspection, remembrance, and the strengthening of bonds:

◆ **Thanksgiving and Harvest Celebrations**: In autumn, as we gather to give thanks for the bounty of the land, smudging our homes and the harvested crops with incense made from cinnamon, clove, and dried apple invites abundance and blessings into our stores and lives.

◆ **Ancestral Remembrance**: Samhain, with its thin veil between worlds, is a poignant time for honoring our ancestors. Incense crafted from mugwort and cedar, known for their protective and visionary properties, can facilitate communication with the spirit realm and invite ancestral wisdom and guidance.

◆ **Welcoming Winter's Rest**: The winter solstice, or Yule, is a time of quiet and reflection. Smudging with pine, spruce, and birch bark can purify the home and hearth, symbolizing the letting go of the old year and the welcome of the new, with its promise of returning light.

Community and Solitary Practices

Smoke magic is adaptable to both community celebrations and solitary rituals, allowing for a deeply personal connection to the seasonal energies:

◆ **Community Celebrations**: In communal settings, large smudge sticks or incense burners can be used to purify and bless the gathering space, participants, and festival icons. Collective rituals, where each participant adds herbs to a communal fire or incense blend, can foster a sense of unity and shared intention.

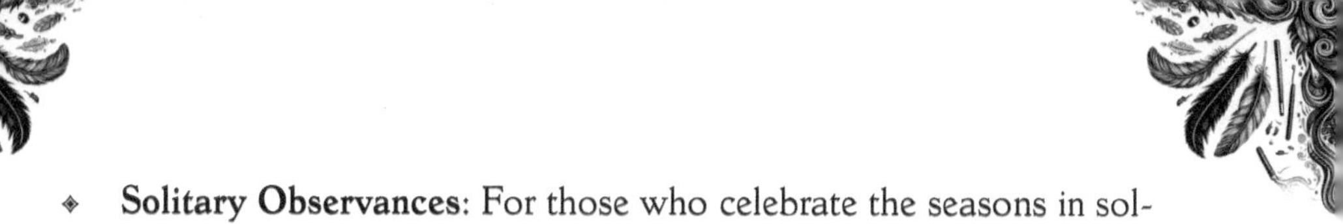

- **Solitary Observances**: For those who celebrate the seasons in solitude, creating personal incense blends based on the individual's connection to the land and the specific energies of the season can be a meditative practice. Solitary smudging rituals can focus on personal purification, protection, and the setting of intentions for the coming cycle.

By embracing the art of smoke magic in our observance of the seasonal festivals, we not only honor the traditions of those who walked these Appalachian paths before us but also deepen our own connection to the cycles of nature and the landscape we call home. Whether in the joyous gatherings of midsummer or the reflective quiet of midwinter, the use of incense and smudging serves as a profound testament to the enduring rhythms of the earth and the ever-renewing cycle of life.

Spring Seed Blessing Smudging Ritual

In the gentle embrace of dawn, as the Appalachian hills awaken with the tender hues of early spring, a sacred ritual unfolds to bless the seeds that will soon nestle into the nurturing earth. This Spring Seed Blessing Smudging Ritual draws upon the delicate energies of early blooming herbs, such as lavender and chamomile, to infuse the seeds with the promise of growth and the anticipation of a fruitful harvest. The rising smoke, carrying the fragrance of these tender herbs, symbolizes the vital force stirring within the seeds, ready to unfold in the warmth of the coming seasons.

Materials Needed:

- **Lavender and Chamomile Incense Blend**: Craft an incense blend combining the soothing and purifying properties of lavender with the gentle, protective energy of chamomile. This blend will serve to purify the seeds and carry your intentions for their growth.

- **A Feather or Fan**: Utilized to spread the incense smoke gently over the seeds, symbolizing the caress of the spring breeze and the breath of life awakening in nature.

- **A Fireproof Bowl or Shell**: To hold the burning incense safely, grounding your ritual in the nurturing embrace of the earth, from which all growth emerges.

Preparation: Select a tranquil time in the early morning, when the world is still and the first light of day begins to touch the earth. Prepare

your space by opening it to the fresh, cool air of spring, setting a stage for renewal and new beginnings.

Crafting the Incense Blend:

1. **Blending with Intent**: On a clean surface, combine the dried lavender and chamomile, herbs known for their association with peace, healing, and protection. Their scents are a harbinger of spring's gentle unfolding and the nurturing energies needed for the seeds to thrive.

2. **Uniting Fragrance and Vitality**: As you mix the herbs, imbue them with your intentions for the seeds—health, vitality, and abundance. Each stir of the blend is a meditation on the cycle of growth and the nurturing power of the earth.

The Ritual:

1. **Awakening of Potential**: Light your lavender and chamomile incense, allowing it to smolder and weave a tapestry of fragrant smoke. Place it within your fireproof container as a beacon of growth and potential.

2. **Benediction over Seeds**: Arrange the seeds you wish to bless before you, using the feather or fan to waft the smoke gently over them. As you do so, articulate your hopes and blessings for the seeds, such as, "With the essence of lavender and chamomile, I bless these seeds with the promise of growth, protection, and abundance."

3. **Circle of Life Affirmation**: Move around your space, carrying the incense to each corner, inviting the energies of renewal and creation to permeate your home, symbolizing the preparation of the environment that will nurture the seeds to fruition.

4. **Harmony with the Earth**: Conclude by holding the container of incense close to the earth, whether in your garden or near your planting pots, acknowledging the deep connection between the seeds and the soil, the giver of all life.

5. **Seal of Vitality**: Finish the ritual by sealing the incense container, allowing the last wisps of smoke to rise, carrying your intentions skyward, mingling with the universal energies that sustain all life.

Closing the Ritual: In the quiet aftermath of the ritual, embrace the sense of calm and readiness that fills your space. Offer gratitude for

the forthcoming growth, to the nurturing spirits of the earth, and to the lavender and chamomile for their blessings. Safely extinguish the incense, knowing that its essence has imbued the seeds with the vitality and promise of the coming harvest.

This Spring Seed Blessing Smudging Ritual, woven from the essence of the Appalachian spring, is a profound act of connection—not only to the earth and its cycles but to the very essence of life itself. Through the careful selection of herbs and the mindful practice of smudging, we honor the potential within each seed, celebrating the continuous dance of growth, renewal, and abundance that defines our existence.

SOLITARY SEASONAL SMUDGING RITUAL

In the hushed serenity of dawn, as the first light caresses the rolling Appalachian landscape, shrouded in a veil of mist, a sacred moment of communion unfolds. This Solitary Seasonal Smudging Ritual is a personal journey, a solitary dance with the elements, guided by the rhythms of the earth and the whispering spirits of the land. It is a time for personal purification, for setting protective boundaries, and for planting the seeds of intentions that will grow with the season's cycle.

Materials Needed:

- **Personal Incense Blend**: Craft your incense blend using herbs that resonate with you and the current season. This could be a mix of white sage for purification, lavender for tranquility, and a personal herb that connects you to the Appalachian landscape or the specific energy of the season.

- **A Feather or Fan**: To gently guide the sacred smoke, symbolizing the element of air and your personal dialogue with the spirit world.

- **A Fireproof Bowl or Shell**: Representing the earth, this vessel will safely cradle the burning herbs, grounding your ritual in the physical and spiritual nourishment of the land.

Preparation: Select a time of quiet introspection, ideally at the break of dawn when the world is still, and the threshold between night and day blurs. Prepare your sacred space by opening it to the embrace of the early morning air, inviting the purity and freshness of the new day.

Crafting the Incense Blend:

1. **Consecration of Herbs**: Lay out your chosen herbs on a clean cloth. Each herb is a companion on your journey, selected for its properties and the personal significance it holds for you. White sage clears the space, lavender soothes the soul, and your chosen herb connects your spirit to the current season.

2. **Blending with Purpose**: As you mix your herbs, infuse them with your intentions. This blend is a reflection of your inner landscape, a tool for transformation tailored to your needs and aspirations.

The Ritual:

1. **Igniting Your Intentions**: Light your personalized incense, allowing it to smolder and awaken the vibrant energies of the herbs. Place it in your fireproof container, letting it become a beacon of your inner light and purpose.

2. **Sanctifying Your Sanctuary**: Stand at the threshold of your space, feather in hand, and gently waft the smoke around you, creating a circle of protection and purity. As you do this, articulate your intentions for the season, whether they be for growth, healing, or renewal.

3. **Heart and Hearth Cleansing**: Move to the center of your space, the heart of your personal sanctuary. Allow the smoke to envelop you, purifying your aura and the core of your being. Here, in the silence of your solitude, reaffirm your connection to the hearth of your spirit, declaring, "In this sacred space, I am aligned with the harmony, strength, and peace of the earth."

4. **Intimate Invocation**: Navigate your space, visiting each corner, each nook that holds a piece of your story. With each step, let the smoke trail your movements, cleansing, and consecrating your personal haven, ensuring that every inch is touched by your intentions and blessings.

5. **Seal of Solitude**: Conclude your ritual by returning to the heart of your space. With a final flourish of your feather, send the remaining smoke upwards, a signal to the universe of your readiness to embrace the season's gifts and challenges.

   Closing the Ritual: In the aftermath of your smudging, bask in the renewed sense of peace and clarity that now fills your space. Offer a

silent word of thanks to the herbs, the land, and the guiding spirits of the Appalachian tradition. Carefully extinguish your incense, knowing that the essence of your intentions has been woven into the fabric of the universe.

This Solitary Seasonal Smudging Ritual, while deeply personal, is rooted in the ancient traditions of Appalachia, a testament to the enduring connection between the land and the individual spirit. It is a ritual of empowerment, a declaration of one's intentions, and a celebration of the solitary path, guided by the wisdom of the earth and the cycles that govern all life.

CONCLUDING THOUGHTS

As we draw the curtains on Chapter 7, "Incense for the Seasons," we reflect on the harmonious dance between the earth's cycles and the ancient art of smoke magic, deeply rooted in Appalachian tradition. This chapter has been a journey through the Wheel of the Year, guided by the fragrant whispers of incense and the purifying embrace of smudge smoke, each turn revealing the intimate connection between the land's rhythms and our spiritual practices.

In crafting seasonal incense blends and smudging rituals, we've tapped into the essence of each season— from the awakening bloom of spring to the lush abundance of summer, from the reflective bounty of autumn to the introspective stillness of winter. Each recipe, each ritual, is a testament to the profound impact of aligning our spiritual practices with the natural world, honoring the energies that govern the cycle of growth, harvest, decline, and renewal.

Celebrating the seasonal festivals with smoke magic has offered us a way to not only honor the traditions of those who have walked these Appalachian paths before us but also to forge our own connections with the cycles of nature. By weaving incense and smudging into the fabric of these celebrations, we've created sacred moments of communion, connection, and renewal—each one a thread in the rich tapestry of Appalachian folk magic.

As we move forward, let us carry the wisdom of this chapter in our hearts and practices. May the scents of our seasonal incense blends linger as a reminder of the earth's abundance and the spirits' guidance. And may our smudging rituals continue to purify, protect, and sanctify, bridging the gap between the physical and the spiritual, the earth and the ether.

Chapter 8:
Smoke in Healing and Protection

USING INCENSE AND SMUDGE STICKS IN HEALING RITUALS AND PROTECTIVE MAGIC

In the heart of the Appalachian mountains, where ancient wisdom whispers through the leaves and streams, the use of smoke in healing rituals and protective magic is a sacred tradition passed down through generations. This chapter, "Smoke in Healing and Protection," unfolds the mystical layers of how smoke from incense and smudge sticks becomes a conduit for wellness and safeguarding, embodying the potent energies of the earth and the ancestors.

Healing Rituals with Smoke

In Appalachian folk practices, smoke serves as a bridge between the physical and spiritual realms, offering a medium through which healing can flow. Central to these practices are the herbs and resins chosen for their intrinsic healing properties, each selected with intention and respect for the ailment at hand.

Healing Herbs and Their Smoke

- **Eucalyptus (Eucalyptus globulus):** Revered for its potent clearing abilities, eucalyptus smoke is often employed in rituals aimed at cleansing the respiratory system. Its sharp, invigorating scent cuts through stagnation, promoting clarity and health.

- **Lavender (Lavandula spp.):** Lavender's gentle, soothing smoke is a balm for the troubled mind and weary spirit. In healing rituals, it is used to calm anxiety, ease insomnia, and restore balance to the emotional body.

Rituals of Smoke Bathing

One of the most intimate forms of smoke healing is the smoke bath, where the individual is enveloped in the healing scents of burning herbs. This practice often involves a quiet, meditative space where the smoke is allowed to wash over the body, carrying away physical and etheric impurities. The person might stand, sit, or lie down while a helper or

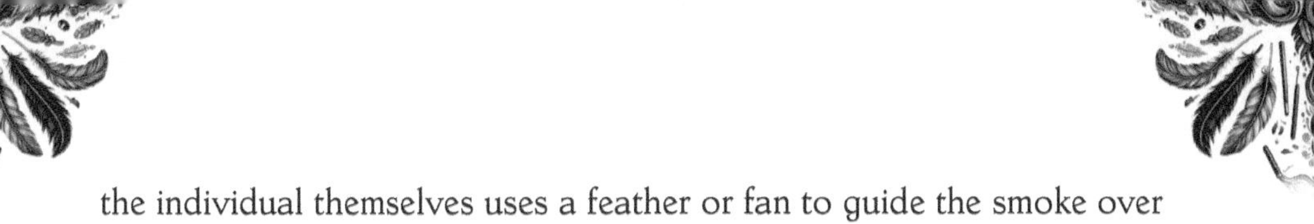

the individual themselves uses a feather or fan to guide the smoke over the body, paying particular attention to areas of discomfort or disease.

Protective Magic with Smoke

Beyond its healing capabilities, smoke is a powerful ally in protective magic. It acts as an invisible shield, a barrier against negativity and harm.

Protective Herbs and Their Smoke

- **Cedar (Juniperus virginiana)**: Cedar smoke is a fortress against negative forces. Its robust, grounding aroma is utilized to fortify homes, sanctify spaces, and offer protection during spiritual work.

- **Black Sage (Salvia mellifera)**: Also known as mugwort, black sage is a guardian herb. Its thick, heady smoke is perfect for warding off evil spirits and negative energies, creating a safe and sacred space.

Casting Protective Circles with Smoke

A foundational protective ritual involves casting a circle with smoke, creating a sacred boundary that neither harm nor malevolence can cross. Starting at the eastern point, the practitioner moves deosil (clockwise), guiding the smoke along the perimeter of the circle, often with a chant or prayer calling in protection from the four corners of the world, the elements, and the guiding spirits of the land.

Smudging for Protection

The act of smudging—burning herbs and passing objects, spaces, or individuals through the smoke—is a potent protective practice. Key to this ritual is the intention behind the smudging:

- **Entrances and Windows**: To safeguard a dwelling, smudging around doors and windows creates a seal against intrusion, both physical and spiritual.

- **Protective Barriers**: Smudging around a person's aura or an object instills a shield, repelling negativity and preventing energetic drains.

In both healing and protection, the magic of smoke is its ability to transform, transmute, and transcend. It carries the prayers of the practitioner, weaving a tapestry of wellness and safety that is both ancient and ever-new. As we delve into these practices, we connect with a lineage of healers and protectors who have long understood the profound alliance between the botanical world and the realms of spirit and magic.

Appalachian Dawn Smoke Bathing Ritual

In the gentle embrace of early morning, as the Appalachian horizon softly glows with the first light of daybreak, a sacred ritual of healing and renewal unfolds. The Ritual of Smoke Bathing, deeply embedded in Appalachian healing traditions, harnesses the gentle power of smoke to cleanse the spirit and soothe the body, offering a profound connection to the healing forces of nature.

Materials Needed:

- **Lavender (Lavandula spp.) Bundle**: A symbol of peace and purification, lavender is gathered from the lush Appalachian fields, revered for its calming and healing properties.

- **Eucalyptus (Eucalyptus globulus) Leaves**: Known for its clear, invigorating aroma, eucalyptus is celebrated for its ability to cleanse the air and support respiratory health.

- **Mint (Mentha spp.) Sprigs**: Mint, with its refreshing and uplifting scent, is used to invigorate the spirit and stimulate healing energies.

- **A Large Feather or Hand Fan**: These tools are employed to gently waft the healing smoke over and around the body, guiding it to areas in need of healing.

- **A Fireproof Container**: This serves as a safe vessel to hold the smoldering herbs, symbolizing the hearth and the nurturing heart of the home.

Preparation: Choose a serene and sacred space, preferably outdoors where the earth's energies are palpable, and the air is fresh with the scent of morning dew. This time, just as the world awakens, is ideal for a smoke bath, as it aligns with the natural rhythms of renewal and rebirth.

Crafting the Healing Bundle:

1. **Foundation of Lavender**: Begin by laying out a lavender bundle on a clean, flat surface. This fragrant herb forms the heart of your healing bundle, setting the tone for peace and restoration.

2. **Layering Eucalyptus**: Gently place eucalyptus leaves atop the lavender. The eucalyptus acts as a layer of purification, bringing clarity and deep cleansing to the ritual.

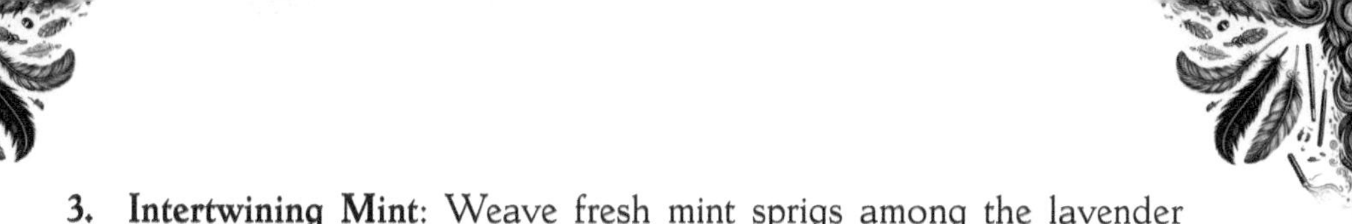

3. **Intertwining Mint**: Weave fresh mint sprigs among the lavender and eucalyptus, introducing a burst of revitalizing energy to the bundle.

4. **Binding the Herbs**: Using natural twine, start at the base of your herb assembly. Secure the end of the twine with your thumb, then wrap it snugly upward, ensuring each turn slightly overlaps the last, to hold the herbs firmly in place.

5. **Securing the Bundle**: Upon reaching the top, wind the twine around several times before descending in a crisscross fashion to the base. Tie a strong knot to secure the bundle. Trim any excess twine and arrange the herbs for a tidy appearance.

The Ritual:

1. **Igniting the Bundle**: Light the herbal bundle, allowing the flames to kiss the herbs briefly before extinguishing them to let the embers glow and smoke. Place the smoldering bundle in your fireproof container.

2. **Cleansing the Aura**: Starting at the crown, use the feather or fan to sweep the smoke gently around your body, moving downward in a fluid, encompassing motion. Envision the smoke as a cleansing waterfall, washing away tension, illness, and negative energy.

3. **Focusing on Afflicted Areas**: Pay special attention to any areas of discomfort or imbalance, enveloping them in the smoke's healing embrace. As you do so, softly chant or hold a silent intention for healing and rejuvenation.

4. **Final Blessing**: Conclude the ritual by allowing the smoke to envelop you one last time, head to toe, in a final blessing. Affirm your gratitude for the healing gifts of the herbs, the earth, and the guiding spirits of Appalachia.

Closing the Ritual: As the ritual draws to a close, feel the lightness and renewed energy within and around you. Offer heartfelt thanks to the sacred plants, the land that nurtures them, and the unseen forces that guide and protect. Carefully extinguish the herbal bundle, preserving it for future healing work.

This Ritual of Smoke Bathing, steeped in the traditions of the Appalachian hearth and home, is a testament to the enduring power of nature's healing gifts. Through this sacred practice, we embrace the

transformative energy of smoke, inviting health, balance, and peace into our lives.

MOUNTAIN GUARDIAN SMOKE CIRCLE RITUAL

In the hush of early morning, when the Appalachian hills are shrouded in the delicate caress of dawn's light, a sacred practice unfolds. The Mountain Guardian Smoke Circle Ritual, a cornerstone of Appalachian protective magic, draws upon the ancient wisdom of the land to forge a shield of smoke around one's sacred space.

Materials Needed:

- **White Sage Bundle (Salvia apiana):** A symbol of purification, harvested with reverence from the Appalachian wilderness.

- **Cedar Branches (Juniperus virginiana):** Embodying strength and sanctuary, these branches weave the resilience of the mountains into the ritual.

- **Sweetgrass Braid (Hierochloe odorata):** Signifying peace and ancestral blessings, sweetgrass binds the ritual with threads of harmony.

- **Feather or Fan:** To guide the sacred smoke with the grace of the wind, whispering protection into every corner.

- **Fireproof Vessel:** A shell or bowl to cradle the burning herbs, grounding the ritual in the stability of the earth.

Preparation: Greet the day in a place of peace, where the first light can touch and sanctify your ritual space. Prepare by opening pathways—windows and doors—to invite the breath of the mountains into your circle.

Binding the Smudge Stick:

1. **Foundation:** On a pure cloth, center your white sage, the heart of your smudge stick, dedicated to cleansing.

2. **Protection:** Overlay with slender cedar branches, their presence a guardian's embrace around the sage.

3. **Harmony:** Weave sweetgrass around your sage and cedar, intertwining peace and ancestral wisdom.

4. **Unity:** Bind your bundle with natural twine, wrapping from base to tip, each layer a promise of protection.

5. **Sealing:** At the pinnacle, wind the twine in a crisscross back to the base, tying a knot that anchors your intentions.

The Ritual:

1. **Light of Intention:** Ignite the smudge stick, let it burn, then blow it out to smolder. Nestle it in your fireproof vessel.

2. **Circle of Dawn:** At the eastern edge, begin your circle, moving deosil with the smoke as your guide, encircling your sacred space with chants or prayers that invoke protection from all realms.

3. **Guardians' Call:** At each cardinal point, pause to call upon the elements, the spirits of the land, and the four winds, asking for their guardianship over your circle.

4. **Veil of Protection:** With feather or fan, direct the smoke over thresholds, around windows, creating a veil that shields against harm.

5. **Heart's Shield:** Conclude in the center, the heart of your space, allowing the smoke to spiral upwards, carrying your protective prayers to the skies.

   Closing the Ritual: With the circle cast, feel the embrace of the mountains' guardianship. Offer gratitude to the sage, cedar, and sweetgrass, to the spirits, to the land. Extinguish the smudge stick, preserving its essence for times when protection is sought.

This ritual, steeped in the Appalachian tradition, crafts not merely a protective circle but a sanctuary, a haven guarded by the forces of nature, imbued with the sacred smoke of the Mountain Guardian.

CRAFTING PROTECTIVE AMULETS AND CHARMS WITH INFUSED SMOKE

In the heart of Appalachia, where ancient forests whisper and the mountains hold secrets, there exists a time-honored tradition of weaving protective magic into tangible forms. Among these sacred practices, the crafting of amulets and charms infused with the potent energies of smoke stands as a testament to the region's deep spiritual heritage. This process, rooted in the lore of the land, transforms simple objects into powerful guardians, each carrying the essence of protection through the smoke's embrace.

Infusing Amulets with Smoke

The act of infusing amulets with smoke is a delicate and intentional ritual, requiring a profound connection to the materials and the protective intentions they are meant to embody. This sacred process often begins in the serene twilight hours, where the boundary between worlds thins, and intentions manifest with clarity.

1. **Selecting the Amulet:** Begin by choosing an amulet that speaks to your spirit, be it a stone worn smooth by the waters of a mountain stream, a piece of driftwood shaped by the wind, or a cloth dyed with the hues of the earth. The amulet's natural affinity for absorbing energies makes it an ideal vessel for protection.

2. **Preparing the Sacred Space:** In a quiet space, where the spirits of the land bear witness, prepare your altar with elements that resonate with protection—iron for strength, thorns for defense, or a circle of salt to purify.

3. **Igniting the Sacred Smoke:** Light your bundle of white sage, cedar, or sweetgrass, letting the flames kiss the herbs before blowing them to a smolder. The smoke that rises carries your protective intentions into the very fabric of the amulet.

4. **The Rite of Infusion:** Holding your amulet over the smoldering embers, allow the smoke to envelop it, whispering your intentions for protection, strength, and guardianship. Visualize the smoke as a cloak, wrapping the amulet in layers of impenetrable energy.

5. **Sealing the Essence:** Conclude the infusion by placing the amulet within a fireproof container, letting it bask in the smoke's remnants until the embers fade. This final step seals the protective energies within, making the amulet a beacon of safeguarding.

Materials and Construction

The materials chosen for protective amulets and charms are as varied as the landscapes from which they come, each imbued with its own energy and significance.

- **Porous Stones:** Stones such as pumice or lava rock, with their myriad of cavities, excel in holding smoke's essence. They can be etched with runes or symbols of protection, such as the triquetra or pentacle, to enhance their power.

- **Sacred Woods:** Bits of driftwood, branches of rowan, or slices of oak carry within them the strength of the trees they once were. Carve these woods with protective sigils or bind them with red thread to ward off harm.

- **Herbal Bundles:** Create small sachets filled with protective herbs like mugwort, blackthorn, or nettles. These bundles can be passed through smoke and carried as charms, each herb adding its strength to the wearer's defense.

Activation and Maintenance

The activation of a smoke-infused amulet or charm is a deeply personal ritual, marking the moment when the item transitions from a simple object to a guardian of one's spirit.

1. **The Ritual of Activation:** Under the light of a waxing moon, hold your amulet within your hands, closing your eyes to visualize a shield of light emanating from within it. Recite incantations of protection, or simply state your intention for the amulet to be a guardian against all that would do harm.

2. **Maintenance of Power:** To maintain the amulet's potency, it should be re-infused with smoke on significant days—solstices, equinoxes, or the new moon. This regular recharging ensures that the amulet's protective energies remain vibrant and strong.

3. **The Bond of Spirit:** Remember, the true power of these amulets lies not just in the smoke, the symbols, or the materials, but in the bond forged between the item and its bearer. It is this connection,

nurtured with respect and belief, that awakens the deepest magic of protection.

In the crafting of smoke-infused amulets and charms, we weave together the ancient wisdom of the Appalachian spirits, the natural strength of the land, and the deep well of our intentions. These sacred items serve as a reminder of our connection to the world around us, a tangible manifestation of the protective forces that guide and guard us on our journey.

CRAFTING A PROTECTION AMULET WITH INFUSED SMOKE FROM SACRED WOODS

In the early light of dawn, when the mist hugs the contours of the Appalachian landscape and the first rays of the sun whisper through the leaves, a sacred practice unfolds. This ritual, rooted in the wisdom of the mountains and the ancient guardianship of the forests, involves crafting a protection amulet from the sacred woods that stand as silent sentinels over these ancient lands.

Materials Needed:

- **Sacred Woods:** Choose a piece of driftwood, a branch of rowan, or a slice of oak. These woods, revered for their strength and protective qualities, form the heart of your amulet.

- **White Sage Bundle:** For purification and to infuse the wood with protective energies.

- **Cedar Branches:** To envelop your amulet in strength and resilience.

- **Sweetgrass Braid:** To imbue your amulet with harmony and the blessing of the ancestors.

- **Natural Twine or Cotton String:** To bind the elements together, symbolizing unity and connection.

- **Feather or Fan:** To direct the sacred smoke during the infusion process.

- **Fireproof Bowl or Shell:** To hold the smoldering herbs safely.

Preparation: Select a time of day when peace reigns, preferably at dawn's first light. Open your windows and doors to welcome the cleansing mountain air, preparing your space for this sacred act.

Binding the Amulet:

1. **Laying the Foundations:** On a clean cloth, lay out your chosen piece of sacred wood. This wood will become the vessel for your protective intentions.

2. **Carving Protective Sigils:** Gently carve protective sigils or symbols onto the wood. Choose symbols that resonate with your need for protection, such as runes of warding, the eye of Horus for vigilance, or the pentacle for elemental protection.

3. **Infusing with Cedar and Sweetgrass:** Place cedar branches and sweetgrass around your wooden amulet. The cedar, symbolizing eternal strength, and sweetgrass, calling in peace, form a protective embrace around the wood.

4. **Securing the Amulet:** Bind the elements together with your twine or string. Start at the base, wrapping upwards in a spiral, ensuring each layer firmly secures the herbs to the wood. Finish with a sturdy knot at the top, trimming any excess.

The Ritual:

1. **Ignition of Intent:** Light your white sage bundle, allowing it to catch fire briefly before gently blowing it out, leaving it to smolder. Place it in your fireproof container.

2. **Enveloping the Amulet in Smoke:** Using your feather or fan, waft the purifying smoke over your amulet. As the smoke swirls and dances, visualize it penetrating the wood, the sigils, infusing them with protective energies.

3. **Invocation of Protection:** Holding the amulet within the smoke, recite your invocation of protection. You might say, "With sage, cedar, and sweetgrass, I bind protection into this amulet. May it shield me (or the bearer) from harm and ward off all negativity."

4. **Final Blessing:** Conclude the ritual by passing the amulet through the smoke one final time, sealing in the protective magic. Whisper your thanks to the elements, the plants, and the spirits of the land for their guardianship and blessing.

Closing the Ritual: As you extinguish the sage, feel the protective energies settled within your amulet. Carry it with you or place it in a sacred space, knowing it is charged with the strength of the Appalachian forests, the purity of the sage, and the harmony of the sweetgrass.

This amulet now stands as a guardian, a sacred talisman crafted in the tranquil beauty of dawn, beneath the watchful eyes of the ancient Appalachian spirits.

Crafting Herbal Protection Sachets with Infused Smoke

In the quietude of dawn, as the Appalachian wilderness awakens with a gentle embrace of mist and the first light of daybreak, a revered ritual unfolds. This sacred practice, deeply entrenched in the traditions of the Appalachian homestead, involves the creation of herbal protection sachets, a blend of the mountains' most potent protective herbs, wrapped in the nurturing energies of smoke to serve as guardians for those who carry them.

Materials Needed:

- **Herbal Selection:** Gather protective herbs like mugwort for psychic protection, blackthorn for repelling negativity, and nettles for warding off harm. These herbs, sourced with reverence from the Appalachian wilds, form the essence of your protection sachets.

- **White Sage Bundle:** Symbolic of cleansing and purity, to imbue the sachets with protective energies.

- **Cedar Branches:** Reflecting the mountain's enduring strength, offering additional protection to the sachets.

- **Sweetgrass Braid:** To infuse the sachets with peace, harmony, and ancestral blessings.

- **Natural Fabric Pouches:** Small cloth pouches to hold the herbal blend, serving as the physical vessel for the sachets.

- **Natural Twine or Cotton String:** For sealing the pouches, symbolizing the binding of protective energies.

- **Feather or Fan:** To guide the sacred smoke over the sachets, embedding them with the intended energies.

- **Fireproof Bowl or Shell:** To contain the burning herbs safely during the ritual.

Preparation: Set aside a time of peace, preferably at the break of dawn, when the world is still and the air is fresh. Allow the gentle

breeze to purify your space, readying it for the sacred act of crafting your sachets.

Crafting the Herbal Sachets:

1. **Selecting the Herbs:** On a clean surface, lay out your chosen herbs. Reflect on the protective qualities of each, focusing on your intention to shield and safeguard.

2. **Filling the Pouches:** Carefully place a balanced blend of mugwort, blackthorn, and nettles into each fabric pouch. The combination of these herbs creates a potent shield against negativity and harm.

3. **Sealing with Intent:** Draw the pouches closed with natural twine or cotton string, securing them with a knot. As you tie each pouch, envision the knot as a seal, locking in the protective energies.

The Ritual:

1. **Igniting the Sage:** Light your white sage bundle, allowing it to catch fire briefly before gently extinguishing the flame, letting the embers smolder. Place it within your fireproof container.

2. **Infusing the Sachets with Smoke:** Using your feather or fan, waft the purifying smoke over each herbal sachet. Visualize the smoke permeating the fabric, the herbs, embedding them with a protective aura.

3. **Blessing of Protection:** Holding a sachet within the smoke, articulate your protective blessing, perhaps stating, "With sage, cedar, and sweetgrass, I cloak this charm in protection. May it serve as a guardian, deflecting harm and embracing the bearer with safety."

4. **Empowering Each Space:** Proceed to move through your living space, gently shaking each sachet to release its essence. Focus on doorways, windows, and any area that feels in need of an energetic shield, reciting, "By the power of these sacred herbs, I fortify this space against all that does not serve."

5. **Ancestral Acknowledgment:** To conclude, pass the sachets once more through the smoke, calling in the goodwill and protection of your ancestors and the spirit of the land, affirming, "Guided by the ancients and the wisdom of the earth, these charms are charged with protection."

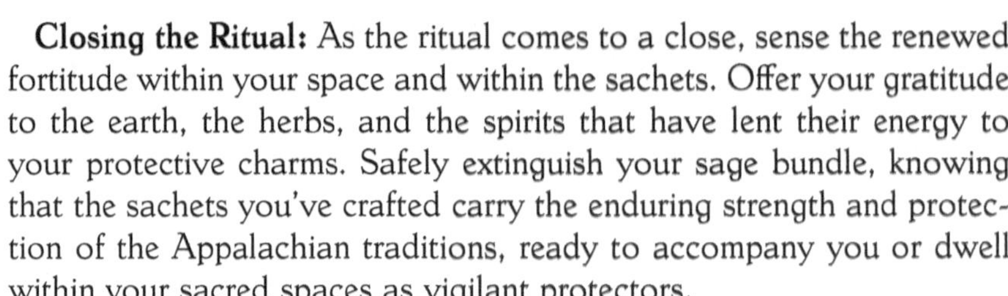

Closing the Ritual: As the ritual comes to a close, sense the renewed fortitude within your space and within the sachets. Offer your gratitude to the earth, the herbs, and the spirits that have lent their energy to your protective charms. Safely extinguish your sage bundle, knowing that the sachets you've crafted carry the enduring strength and protection of the Appalachian traditions, ready to accompany you or dwell within your sacred spaces as vigilant protectors.

Concluding Thoughts

As we draw Chapter 8: "Smoke in Healing and Protection" to a close, we've journeyed through the mystical landscape of Appalachian smoke magic, exploring its profound applications in healing and safeguarding the spirit, body, and environment. This chapter has illuminated the traditional practices of using incense and smudge sticks not just as tools for aromatic pleasure, but as potent allies in rituals of healing and protective magic. We've delved into the heart of Appalachian wisdom, uncovering how the simple act of burning sacred herbs can weave a tapestry of protection around us and infuse our beings with restorative energies.

The crafting of protective amulets and charms with smoke-infused materials stands as a testament to the ingenuity and deep spiritual connection of Appalachian practitioners. These practices bridge the tangible and the ethereal, embodying the belief that the essence of the earth, when merged with human intention and the elemental force of fire, can create powerful talismans to guide and protect us.

"Sacred Smoke and Mountain Spirits" aims not only to preserve these ancient traditions but also to offer them as a gift to those who seek a deeper connection with the natural world and its unseen forces. In embracing these practices, we honor the legacy of countless generations who have found solace, protection, and healing in the smoke of their sacred fires.

As you, the reader, continue to explore the pages of this book and the practices within, may you find not only knowledge but also a profound sense of communion with the spirits of the Appalachian mountains. May the smoke from your rituals rise high, carrying your intentions to the heavens, and may the protection and healing it brings be a source of comfort and strength in your journey.

Chapter 9:
Communicating with the Spirits

INCORPORATING SMOKE IN RITUALS TO COMMUNICATE WITH ANCESTORS AND THE SPIRITS OF THE LAND

In the Appalachian tradition, smoke serves as more than just a ceremonial tool; it acts as a conduit for communication with the unseen world. The practice of using smoke to reach out to ancestors and the spirits of the land is deeply rooted in the belief that these entities play an active role in the lives of the living. This chapter delves into the sacred art of incorporating smoke in rituals designed to bridge the gap between our physical reality and the spiritual realm, offering guidance on how to conduct these rituals with reverence and respect.

Smoke as a Spiritual Conduit

Smoke, with its ethereal qualities, has always been seen as a natural medium for spiritual communication. Its ability to ascend from the earthly plane to the heavens symbolizes the soul's journey after death, making it an ideal messenger between the worlds. In Appalachian lore, smoke is not merely a byproduct of fire but a sacred breath that carries the whispers of the living to the ears of the spirits.

Ritual Framework

Setting the Sacred Space

The first step in a ritual involving smoke is to establish a sacred space. This space acts as a threshold between worlds, a place where the veil thins and communication is possible. It can be anywhere the practitioner feels a strong connection to the spiritual realm, be it a secluded spot in the woods, a home altar, or any place that holds personal significance. Cleansing this area with smoke from white sage or cedar before beginning the ritual is common practice, purifying the space of any lingering energies that might interfere with the communication.

Selecting the Medium

The choice of incense or herbs is crucial in these rituals. Each plant carries its own energy and specific associations with different types of spirits. Tobacco, for example, is traditionally used for ancestral commu-

nication due to its sacred status among many Native American tribes, whose influences permeate Appalachian spiritual practices. Sweetgrass, known for its sweet, calming scent, is often burned to invite the positive energy of land spirits, facilitating a harmonious dialogue.

The Ritual Act

The ritual itself begins with lighting the incense or smudge stick and allowing it to smolder, producing the smoke that will carry the practitioner's messages. Participants might then use a feather or fan to direct the smoke, guiding it to fill the space and envelop any objects or symbols representing the spirits being communicated with. As the smoke rises, the practitioner vocalizes their intentions, prayers, or questions, speaking directly to the spirits. The language used is less important than the sincerity and emotion behind the words, as these are what truly imbue the smoke with the power to reach the spiritual realm.

Closing the Ritual

Concluding the ritual involves thanking the spirits for their presence and any guidance they have provided. This can be done through verbal expressions of gratitude or the offering of gifts, such as food, drink, or other items of significance. It's essential to close the sacred space, acknowledging the end of the communication and the return to ordinary reality. This can be achieved by a final smudging, grounding exercises, or simply declaring the ritual complete.

Respectful Practices

Engaging in smoke rituals to communicate with spirits requires not only knowledge of the proper steps but also a deep respect for the entities involved. Practitioners must approach these rituals with humility, acknowledging the autonomy and power of the spirits. Consent is paramount; just as one would ask permission before entering someone's home, it's crucial to seek the spirits' willingness to communicate.

Interpreting the responses received during these rituals can be challenging. Signs may come in various forms: a sudden insight, a dream, or changes in the natural environment. Patience and openness to these subtle messages are key, as is the willingness to accept that some questions may remain unanswered.

In crafting this chapter, the intention is to honor the rich Appalachian tradition of smoke communication with the spiritual realm. By following these guidelines, practitioners can forge a deeper connection with

the ancestors and spirits of the land, enriching their spiritual practice and fostering a greater understanding of the world beyond our own.

Appalachian Spirit Whisper Smudging Ritual

In the serene embrace of early morning, when the first light of dawn gently brushes the peaks and valleys of the Appalachian landscape, a sacred ritual unfolds. This ritual, rooted in the ancient traditions of Appalachia, is dedicated to connecting with the spiritual realm, seeking guidance, wisdom, and blessings from ancestors and the spirits of the land.

Materials Needed:

- **Tobacco Leaves (Nicotiana tabacum)**: A revered plant known for its use in communication with the ancestors, offering its smoke as a gift to the spirit world.

- **Mountain Mint (Pycnanthemum spp.)**: Symbolizing clarity and insight, mountain mint sharpens the senses and opens the pathways to the spiritual realm.

- **Dogwood Branches (Cornus florida)**: A tree sacred to the Appalachian region, representing protection and the connection between heaven and earth.

- **A Feather or Fan**: To gently guide the smoke, symbolizing the presence of the spirits and the element of air.

- **A Fireproof Bowl or Shell**: To hold the burning herbs safely, grounding the ritual in the stability of the earth.

   Preparation: Choose a time of quiet introspection, when the world is still, and the heart is open to receiving messages from beyond. Prepare your space by opening windows and doors, inviting the breath of the earth to purify and renew.

Binding the Smudge Stick:

1. **Laying the Foundations**: Arrange a clean cloth before you, placing tobacco leaves at its center, laying the groundwork for spiritual communication.

2. **Adding Mountain Mint**: Layer mountain mint atop the tobacco, infusing the bundle with its crisp, clear essence.

3. **Incorporating Dogwood**: Place slender dogwood branches around the tobacco and mint, weaving in the protective energies of this revered tree.

4. **Securing the Bundle**: Bind the herbs and branches together with a natural twine, holding the intention of unity and connection as you wrap the string around the bundle, ensuring each layer supports the next.

5. **Final Blessing**: Once secured, hold the bundle aloft, offering a prayer of thanks to the plants for their sacrifice and to the spirits for their forthcoming guidance.

The Ritual:

1. **Ignition of Intent**: Ignite the smudge stick, allowing the flame to kiss the herbs before extinguishing it to let the embers glow. Cradle it within your fireproof vessel.

2. **Calling the Spirits**: At the threshold of your space, use the feather or fan to waft the smoke into the corners of the room, calling upon the ancestors and land spirits with a heartfelt chant or song that resonates with your intention.

3. **Circle of Communication**: Slowly walk the perimeter of your room or space, creating a circle of smoke that envelopes you, a sacred boundary within which only truth and spirit may dwell.

4. **Heart to Spirit**: Settle in the heart of your space, allowing the smoke to envelop you fully. Here, in the silence, speak your prayers, questions, or thoughts to the spirits, letting the smoke carry your words to the unseen.

5. **Listening**: Sit in stillness, allowing the messages of the spirits to fill the space, listening with your heart for their subtle whispers.

Closing the Ritual: As the smoke clears, express your gratitude to the spirits for their presence and wisdom. Carefully extinguish the smudge stick, preserving it for future dialogues. Reflect on the experience, journaling any insights or messages received.

This ritual, steeped in the heritage of the Appalachian mountains, serves as a bridge to the spiritual realm, offering a means of communication with the forces that guide and protect us. Through the sacred act of smudging, we honor our ancestors and the spirits of the land, weaving their wisdom into the fabric of our lives.

Appalachian Spirit Clearing Smudging Ritual

In the serene twilight of evening, as shadows dance across the Appalachian landscape and the sky turns a deep indigo, a sacred ritual unfolds. The Appalachian Spirit Clearing Smudging Ritual is a venerable tradition, dedicated to purifying spaces of lingering spirits and energies. Harnessing the potent essences of the mountain's flora, this ritual forms a harmonious blend of herbs that cleanse and sanctify, reinstating peace and serenity.

Materials Needed:

- **Black Sage (Salvia mellifera) Bundle:** Known for its strong protective and cleansing properties, black sage is revered for its ability to expel negative spirits.

- **Pine (Pinus spp.) Needles:** For resilience and purification, embodying the enduring spirit of the Appalachian forests.

- **Rosemary (Rosmarinus officinalis) Sprigs:** Symbolizing remembrance and protection, rosemary bridges the physical and spiritual worlds.

- **An Owl Feather or Traditional Fan:** To gently guide the purifying smoke, symbolizing wisdom and the depth of night.

- **A Cauldron or Fireproof Container:** Representing the element of fire, transforming and renewing energies.

Preparation: Select an evening where the moon is waning, symbolizing decrease and removal. Ventilate the area, inviting the cool mountain breeze to aid in the cleansing process.

Binding the Smudge Stick:

1. **Foundation:** On a piece of natural cloth, lay the black sage as the base for deep cleansing.

2. **Strength and Purification:** Add pine needles over the sage, infusing the bundle with resilience.

3. **Memory and Protection:** Intersperse rosemary sprigs, weaving in protection and remembrance.

4. **Securing the Bundle:** Bind with a dark thread, starting from the base, tightly winding upward, then back down in a reverse pattern. Knot securely, embodying intention in each twist.

The Ritual:

1. **Ignition of Intent:** Ignite the smudge stick, allowing it to catch fire momentarily before extinguishing to smolder. Rest it within the cauldron.

2. **Boundary Setting:** At the entrance, commence with the owl feather or fan, wafting smoke along the doorframe, voicing, "With black sage, pine, and rosemary, I cleanse this threshold; only peace may reside within."

3. **Core Sanctification:** Proceed to the heart of the dwelling, encircling the primary living space, chanting, "Purify this hearth with ancient woods, let shadows depart and only good remain."

4. **Sequestered Spaces:** Methodically navigate each room, focusing on secluded areas, visualizing all residual spirits being guided away, affirming, "By the wisdom of the owl and the depth of the night, be at peace and journey forth from this site."

5. **Final Blessing:** Complete the ritual in the central space, swirling sweetgrass to invite positive energy, declaring, "With sweetgrass, I seal this home in harmony, embraced by tranquility."

Closing the Ritual: As the ritual concludes, sense the tranquility restored. Offer thanks to the sage, pine, and rosemary, the Appalachian spirits, and the wisdom of the owl. Carefully extinguish the smudge stick, preserving it for future needs.

This ritual, rooted in the traditions of Appalachia, transforms your space into a sanctuary of peace. Through the meticulous binding of the herbs, you intertwine the forces of nature, crafting not just a tool, but a beacon of protection and purity.

APPALACHIAN TALES OF SPIRIT COMMUNICATION THROUGH SMOKE

In the heart of Appalachia, where the ancient mountains whisper secrets of the old world and the mist veils the thin places between realms, the practice of communicating with the spirit world through smoke is deeply interwoven into the fabric of local folklore and tradition. These tales, passed down through generations, serve not only as a testament to the region's rich spiritual heritage but also as a guide for those seeking to bridge the gap between the physical and the spiritual.

The Whispering Smoke of Old Man Whittaker

Deep in the heart of Appalachia, where ancient forests cloak the mountainside and the air carries whispers of ages past, lived Old Man Whittaker. A recluse by nature, he dwelled in a humble cabin on the forest's edge, far removed from the hustle of town life. Whittaker was a man of the woods, understanding its language and secrets as one born of the earth itself.

Legend has it that Whittaker possessed a unique gift, one that allowed him to commune with the spirits of the forest. On nights when the moon hung full and bright, casting a silver glow over the land, he would kindle a fire outside his cabin. Into the flames, he cast dried herbs he had gathered—sage for purification, sweetgrass for harmony, and tobacco as an offering to the spirits. As the fire crackled and roared, the smoke would rise, thick and heady with the scent of the herbs.

The smoke, under Whittaker's watchful gaze, would begin to dance. It twisted and twirled into the night, forming shapes that only Whittaker could interpret. The spirits of the forest, drawn by the scent of the burning herbs and the sincerity of Whittaker's heart, would speak through these patterns. They offered wisdom, guidance, and sometimes, warnings of things to come.

Whittaker's story teaches us the sacredness of smoke as a bridge between worlds. It reminds us that to communicate with the spirits, one must approach with intention, respect, and an open heart. The rituals he practiced underscore the belief in smoke's power to convey

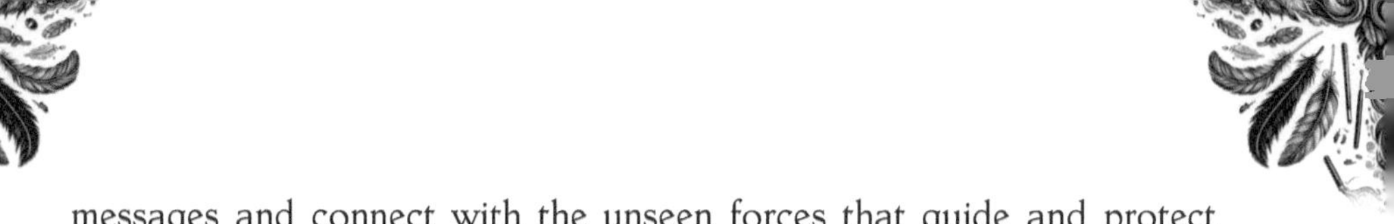

messages and connect with the unseen forces that guide and protect the natural world.

The Veiled Lady of the Mist

On the edges of Appalachian lore, where reality and myth intertwine, the tale of the Veiled Lady of the Mist has been passed down through generations. She is a spectral figure, draped in a misty shroud, her features obscured but her presence undeniably comforting. She is said to appear to travelers lost in the dense Appalachian fog, her form barely distinguishable from the swirling mists around her.

Unlike other tales that warn of malevolent spirits lurking in the shadows, the Veiled Lady's story is one of guidance and protection. She does not speak in words but communicates through the mist, which the locals believe to be akin to sacred smoke. With a gentle nudge or a soft whisper of the wind, she leads the wayward back to their paths, ensuring their safety.

This legend speaks to the profound connection between the people of Appalachia and their environment. The mist, much like smoke, is seen as a medium for spiritual interaction, a natural phenomenon imbued with the power to protect and guide. The Veiled Lady, through her actions, teaches the value of kindness and the protective embrace of the land's spirits.

The Coal Miner's Premonition

In the shadowy depths of Appalachian coal mines, where the earth whispers secrets long forgotten, a tale of foresight and protection emerged. It's a story of a group of miners, hardened by the earth's embrace, yet not immune to the chills of premonition.

On an ordinary dawn, as the miners gathered at the mouth of the mine, a peculiar sight stopped them in their tracks. From the depths of the earth, smoke began to drift, forming an ominous cloud at the entrance. This was no ordinary smoke; it seemed to pulse with an unseen energy, warning of danger lurking within the cavernous depths.

Heeding this warning, the miners stepped back, their instincts aflame with caution. Their decision proved wise when, hours later, the mine collapsed. The incident would have claimed many lives had it not been for the protective message conveyed through the smoke.

This tale underscores the deep respect for signs and omens that permeates Appalachian culture. Smoke, in this story, is not merely a by-

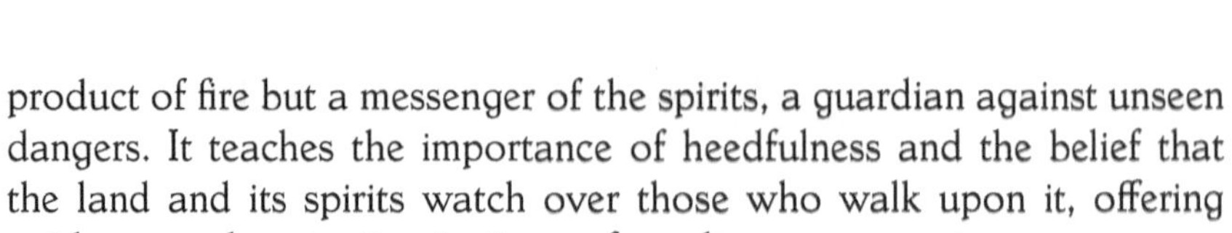

product of fire but a messenger of the spirits, a guardian against unseen dangers. It teaches the importance of heedfulness and the belief that the land and its spirits watch over those who walk upon it, offering guidance and protection in times of need.

Lessons and Insights

These tales, rich in symbolism and meaning, offer profound insights into the Appalachian understanding of the spirit world. They reveal a deep respect for the spirits, an acknowledgment of their presence in everyday life, and the belief that smoke, whether from a fire, incense, or the natural environment, serves as a conduit for communication. The stories teach the importance of interpreting the language of smoke and mist, urging us to pay attention to the subtle messages conveyed through these mediums.

Modern Interpretations

In contemporary practice, these ancient traditions and tales continue to inspire. They remind us of the power of smoke not only as a tool for purification and protection but also as a bridge to the spiritual realm. Modern practitioners can draw from these stories, incorporating smoke rituals into their spiritual practice while adapting them to fit their personal beliefs and the modern context. Whether through the burning of sage, incense, or simply observing the patterns of mist in a forest, the act of seeking communion with the spirit world through smoke is a timeless practice, as relevant today as it was in the days of Old Man Whittaker and the Veiled Lady.

In these Appalachian tales, smoke emerges not just as a physical phenomenon, but as a living, breathing entity that connects us with the spirits of the land, our ancestors, and the unseen forces that guide and shape our lives. They encourage us to approach spirit communication with reverence, to listen more closely to the whispers of the natural world, and to find within the curling tendrils of smoke the ancient wisdom that has long guided the people of Appalachia.

CONCLUDING THOUGHTS

As we draw Chapter 9 to a close, we reflect on the profound wisdom and mystical heritage woven into the Appalachian tradition of smoke communication with the spirit realm. Through the veils of smoke, we've explored the ancient practice of reaching out to ancestors and land spirits, delving into the sacred rituals that allow for such profound connections. The tales and legends shared in these pages, from the whispering smoke of Old Man Whittaker to the guiding mists of the Veiled Lady, encapsulate the deep spiritual bonds that tie the people of Appalachia to their environment and the unseen forces that dwell within it.

This chapter has not only shed light on the methods and practices of spirit communication through smoke but also emphasized the respect, intention, and purity of heart required to engage with such powerful forces. We've seen how smoke, as a spiritual conduit, transcends the physical realm, carrying prayers, intentions, and messages to those who have passed and the spirits that watch over the land. These practices underscore a broader theme of interconnectedness—a reminder that we are part of a larger tapestry of existence, bound to both the earth and the ethereal.

The tales of spirit communication, enriched with the essence of Appalachian folklore, offer more than just accounts of mystical encounters. They provide insights into a way of life deeply attuned to the natural and spiritual worlds, where every mist and wisp of smoke can hold deeper meanings, and the boundaries between worlds are as thin as the mountain air.

As we move forward, carrying the knowledge and stories of this chapter, let us do so with a renewed sense of reverence for the traditions that have allowed us to glimpse into the soul of Appalachia. May the smoke from our fires carry our deepest respects and intentions to the spirits with whom we share this world, and may their wisdom guide us on our path. In honoring these practices, we not only connect with the spirits of the land but also weave our own stories into the rich tapestry of Appalachian lore, ensuring that the sacred smoke continues to rise, bridging worlds and bringing us closer to the mysteries that surround us.

Chapter 10:
Advanced Smoke Magic

Combining Incense and Smudging with Other Magical Practices

In the rich tapestry of Appalachian magical practices, smoke magic holds a revered place, serving not only as a vehicle for cleansing and purification but also as a potent ally in more complex ritualistic workings. Chapter 10 of "Sacred Smoke and Mountain Spirits" delves into the advanced techniques of smoke magic, revealing how it intertwines with other forms of magic to enhance and amplify the practitioner's intentions. This section, in particular, explores the seamless integration of smoke magic with candle magic and sigils, offering practitioners nuanced methods to deepen their magical practice.

Integration with Candle Magic

Candle magic, with its vivid symbolism and accessibility, is a fundamental practice within many magical traditions, including those of the Appalachian region. The flame of a candle represents transformation, light, and the manifestation of will, while smoke serves as the ethereal medium through which our intentions are communicated to the spiritual realms. When combined, they create a powerful synergy that can be harnessed for a variety of magical purposes.

Amplifying Intentions

One of the most straightforward yet profound ways to combine smoke and candle magic is through intention amplification. For instance, in a ritual designed to bolster personal protection, a practitioner might choose a black candle for its ability to absorb negativity. As the candle burns, the practitioner surrounds it with a circle of protective incense, perhaps a blend of cedar, sage, and salt. The rising smoke not only purifies the space but also carries the protective intent upwards, magnifying the candle's power.

This technique can be adapted to various intentions, from love and healing to prosperity and wisdom. The key is to select incense blends that correspond with the candle's purpose, creating a harmonious blend of aromas and energies.

Candle Dressing with Incense Ashes

Another method involves dressing candles with incense ashes, a practice that imbues the candle with the properties of the herbs and resins used in the incense. After burning a specially prepared incense blend, the practitioner collects the ashes and gently rolls the candle in them, focusing on their intention. As the candle burns, it releases the combined energies of the incense and wax, creating a potent focal point for the practitioner's will.

Incorporating Sigils

Sigils, or magical symbols designed to represent and manifest a specific intent, offer another layer of depth to smoke magic. These symbols can be crafted to encapsulate a wide array of desires and goals, from personal growth and protection to love and abundance.

Creating Sigils with Smoke

One of the most visually striking methods of incorporating sigils into smoke magic involves drawing the sigil in the air with the smoke of a smudge stick or incense. The practitioner visualizes the sigil as they move the smoking vessel through the air, tracing the symbol while focusing on their intent. This act not only charges the sigil with the practitioner's will but also with the properties of the herbs or resins being burned.

Inscribing Sigils on Incense

For a more lasting effect, practitioners can inscribe sigils directly onto incense sticks or cones before burning. Using a small pin or needle, the sigil is carefully etched onto the incense. As the incense burns, the sigil is activated, releasing its intent into the universe. This method is particularly effective for spells that require a gradual release of energy, such as those aimed at long-term goals or slow healing processes.

Respectful Practices

It's important to approach these advanced techniques with respect and mindfulness, understanding the significance of each element used in the rituals. The herbs and resins carry the spirits of the plants from which they came, the candles hold the transformative power of fire, and the sigils represent the crystallization of our deepest desires and intentions.

In crafting incense blends or performing rituals that combine these elements, practitioners are advised to work with a clear mind and an

open heart, ensuring that their actions are in harmony with the natural world and their own spiritual path. Whether amplifying intentions with candle magic, inscribing sigils for focused will, or any other advanced technique, the key lies in the mindful and respectful use of smoke as a sacred bridge between the physical and the spiritual.

APPALACHIAN SPIRIT HARMONY RITUAL

In the gentle embrace of dawn, as the Appalachian wilderness awakens with a symphony of colors and sounds, a deeply transformative ritual unfolds. This Layered Ritual combines the ancient art of smudging with the harmonious power of crystals and the resonant vibrations of sound therapy. Drawing from the abundant heart of the mountains, this practice melds the sacred energies of the earth, air, and spirit, fostering an environment of profound healing and protection.

Materials Needed:

- **White Sage Bundle**: A symbol of purification, hand-harvested with reverence from the wilds.

- **Cedar Branches**: Embodying strength and protection, these branches echo the resilience of the mountains.

- **Sweetgrass Braid**: A token of peace, harmony, and ancestral goodwill.

- **Healing Crystals**: Select crystals like amethyst for spiritual connection, clear quartz for amplification, and black tourmaline for protection.

- **Tibetan Singing Bowl or Tuning Fork**: Instruments of sound therapy to weave the element of vibration into the ritual.

- **Feather or Fan**: To guide the sacred smoke, embodying the breath of the spirit.

- **Fireproof Bowl or Shell**: A safe vessel to hold the smoldering herbs, symbolizing the earth's embrace.

Preparation: In the quiet of the morning, when the world is still and the air is fresh, prepare your space. Open the pathways to the natural world by inviting in the crisp mountain air, setting the stage for the ritual.

Binding the Smudge Stick:

1. **Foundation**: On a clean cloth, lay the white sage at the heart of your bundle, intending for purification.

2. **Strength**: Add cedar atop the sage, enveloping it with layers of protection.

3. **Harmony**: Weave sweetgrass around the sage and cedar, infusing the bundle with positive energies.

4. **Unity**: With natural twine, begin at the base, binding the herbs tightly, layer over layer, securing the energies within.

5. **Completion**: At the apex of the bundle, secure your intent with a firm knot, trimming the excess, readying the bundle for the ritual.

The Ritual:

1. **Ignition**: Light the smudge stick, letting it catch flame briefly before allowing it to smolder. Place it within the fireproof container, ready to carry your intentions.

2. **Threshold**: At the entrance of your space, use the feather to spread the smoke, stating, "By sage, cedar, and sweetgrass, this threshold is guarded, welcoming only light and love."

3. **Crystal Activation**: Position your selected crystals around the perimeter of your space or on your person. As the smudge stick burns, gently strike the singing bowl or tuning fork, allowing the vibrations to resonate with the crystals, charging them with protective and healing energies.

4. **Sound Bath**: In the center of your space, envelop yourself in the sound waves emanating from the bowl or fork, letting the vibrations cleanse your aura in tandem with the smoke.

5. **Personal Purification**: Guide the smoke over your body with the fan, focusing particularly on areas in need of healing or release. With each wave of smoke, envision the dissipation of all that no longer serves you, making room for renewal and growth.

6. **Gratitude and Release**: Conclude by weaving sweetgrass smoke through your space, inviting in positive energy and blessings. Offer thanks to the sage, cedar, and sweetgrass, to the crystals and the healing sounds, and to the spirits of the Appalachian lands.

Closing the Ritual: As the ritual comes to a close, feel the space and yourself renewed, cleansed, and vibrantly alive. Offer a final word of thanks to the elements and spirits involved. Extinguish the smudge stick safely, preserving its essence for future rituals.

This Layered Ritual, rooted in Appalachian wisdom, harmonizes the protective forces of nature, the grounding energy of crystals, and the cleansing power of sound. It serves not merely as a practice but as a profound journey of the spirit, embracing the complexities of the natural and ethereal worlds.

APPALACHIAN DAWN HARMONY CEREMONY

In the first light of dawn, where the Appalachian horizon softly blurs with hues of pink and gold, a serene ceremony unfolds, blending the ancient tradition of smudging with the grounding presence of crystals and the ethereal echoes of sound therapy. This Appalachian Dawn Harmony Ceremony is a dance of elements, weaving together the earth's gifts and the ether's whispers into a tapestry of deep tranquility and rejuvenation.

Materials Needed:

- **Mountain Sage Bundle**: Harvested with care from the wild, embodying the spirit of purification.

- **Cedar Twigs**: Representing the enduring strength and protective embrace of the mountain woods.

- **Meadow Sweetgrass Braid**: Symbolizing the gentle flow of peace and the ancestral voices of harmony.

- **Healing Crystals**: Chosen pieces of rose quartz for love and heart healing, smoky quartz for grounding, and lapis lazuli for spiritual insight.

- **Crystal Singing Bowl**: To infuse the ritual with cleansing vibrations, harmonizing with the soul's frequency.

- **Handcrafted Feather Fan**: To spread the sacred smoke with intention, as a gentle caress of the spirit.

- **Stone or Ceramic Basin**: A vessel to cradle the burning herbs, grounding the ceremony in the stability of the earth.

Preparation: Embrace the stillness of the early morning, setting a sacred space where the calm of nature meets the threshold of your dwelling. Let the fresh breath of the Appalachians fill your space, preparing you for the ceremony ahead.

Creating the Smudge Bundle:

- **Core of Purity**: Begin with the mountain sage at the heart, a foundation of cleansing.

- **Layer of Guardianship**: Add the cedar, wrapping it around the sage, offering protection.

- **Weave of Harmony**: Encircle with sweetgrass, binding the elements in unity and peace.

- **Bond of Intent**: Secure the bundle with natural fibers, each wrap a seal of your purpose.

- **Circle of Completion**: Finish with a knot at the top, a symbol of wholeness and readiness.

The Ceremony:

- **Spark of Beginnings**: Ignite the smudge bundle, allowing it to smolder. Nestle it in the basin as a beacon of your intentions.

- **Guardian Passage**: At the entrance, with the fan, disperse the smoke, affirming, "Through sage, cedar, and sweetgrass, this gateway is sanctified, open only to light and love."

- **Circle of Stones**: Position the crystals at key points, forming a protective and empowering boundary. As the smudge emits its essence, strike the singing bowl, aligning the crystal energies with the sacred sounds.

- **Vibrational Embrace**: Stand or sit at the heart of your space, bathing in the sonic waves of the bowl, allowing the sound to intertwine with the smoke, enveloping you in a cocoon of healing frequencies.

- **Purification Path**: With the feather fan, draw the smoke across your being, focusing on areas yearning for release or healing. Envision the smoke lifting burdens, clearing blockages, and revitalizing your spirit.

- **Benediction of Sweetgrass**: To conclude, suffuse your space with sweetgrass smoke, an invitation to positivity and blessings. Express

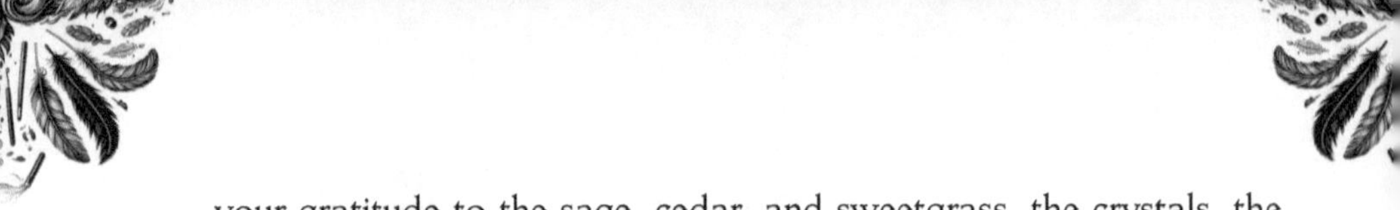

your gratitude to the sage, cedar, and sweetgrass, the crystals, the resonant bowl, and the spirits of the land.

Closing the Ceremony: As the ceremony gently winds down, feel the renewed sense of balance and vibrancy within and around you. Offer a heartfelt thanks to the elements and guardians. Safely extinguish the smudge bundle, preserving its essence for future ceremonies.

This Appalachian Dawn Harmony Ceremony is not just a ritual but a sacred journey that harmonizes the protective energies of nature, the nurturing power of crystals, and the purifying resonance of sound, creating a sanctuary of peace and renewal at the break of day.

APPALACHIAN TWILIGHT FLAME AND SMOKE CEREMONY

As the sun dips below the Appalachian peaks, casting long shadows and painting the sky in shades of orange and indigo, a profound ceremony commences. This Twilight Flame and Smoke Ceremony marries the ancient art of smudging with the timeless magic of candlelight, creating a potent fusion of elements that amplify intentions, particularly for protection and purification.

Materials Needed:

- **Mountain Sage Bundle**: Revered for its purifying properties, carefully harvested from the wild.

- **Cedar Sprigs**: To symbolize and invoke the mountain's protective strength.

- **Sweetgrass Braid**: For calling in peace, harmony, and ancestral support.

- **Protective Candles**: Black for absorbing negativity, white for purity and protection, and red for strength and vitality.

- **Feather or Handcrafted Fan**: To guide and shape the smoke, channeling the spirit's breath.

- **Earthen Bowl or Shell**: A grounded vessel to hold the embering herbs, connecting the ritual to the earth.

Preparation: Embrace the tranquil transition from day to night, setting your sacred space at this powerful threshold moment. Invite the

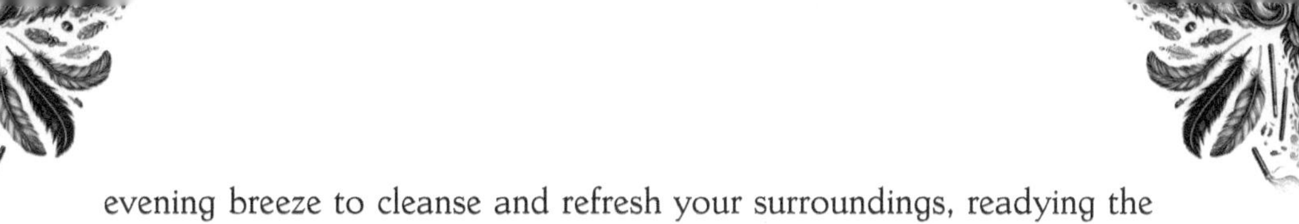

evening breeze to cleanse and refresh your surroundings, readying the space for the ceremony.

Creating the Smudge Bundle:

- **Foundation of Clarity**: Begin with mountain sage at the heart of the bundle, dedicated to cleansing and clarity.

- **Guardian Layer**: Encircle with cedar sprigs, providing a protective barrier and strength.

- **Harmony Weave**: Bind with sweetgrass, creating a harmonious blend of energies.

- **Binding Unity**: Secure with natural twine, each turn reinforcing your intentions.

- **Seal of Intent**: Finalize with a strong knot at the top, completing the preparation with focused intention.

The Ceremony:

- **Spark of Intent**: Ignite the sage bundle, allowing the flames to kiss the herbs before settling into a gentle smolder within the earthen bowl.

- **Candle Vigil**: Light the protective candles, arranging them to form a triangle around the smudging bowl, each flame a beacon of strength, purity, and resilience.

- **Boundary of Light and Smoke**: With the feather or fan, waft the sage smoke around the candle flames, weaving a protective circle that melds the smoke's cleansing power with the candles' radiant energy.

- **Sanctuary Invocation**: Move through your space with the smoldering sage and candlelight, focusing on corners, doorways, and windows. Chant or silently affirm, "By the light of flame and the dance of smoke, this space is sealed from shadow and harm."

- **Heart of the Home**: Center the ceremony in your dwelling's heart, allowing the smoke and candlelight to fill the area with warmth, protection, and clarity.

- **Blessing Infusion**: Conclude by guiding the smoke with your feather or fan over yourself and loved ones, enveloping each in a protec-

tive embrace, while affirming, "Surrounded by light, embraced by the mountain's breath, we stand guarded and pure."

Closing the Ceremony: As the ceremony gently concludes, bask in the serene energy and strengthened defenses of your space. Offer gratitude to the sage, cedar, and sweetgrass, to the elemental forces of fire and air, and to the spirits of the land for their guidance and protection. Carefully extinguish the smudge stick and candles, preserving their essence for future ceremonies.

This Appalachian Twilight Flame and Smoke Ceremony is a sacred confluence of smoke's cleansing spirit and fire's protective might, crafted to fortify and purify your space as day transitions into night, harnessing the potent energies of dusk in the heart of the mountains.

APPALACHIAN SIGIL AND SMOKE EMPOWERMENT RITUAL

In the early hours, as dawn breaks over the Appalachian range, the land whispers secrets of old. Here begins the Sigil and Smoke Empowerment Ritual, a practice intertwining the ancient art of sigil magic with the sacred act of smudging. This ritual draws from the earth's depths, harnessing the power of symbols and smoke to protect, empower, and manifest intentions.

Materials Needed:

- **High Mountain Sage Bundle**: For purification, handpicked from the alpine slopes.

- **Cedar Twigs**: Representing eternal strength, sourced from the heart of ancient forests.

- **Sweetgrass Strands**: Symbolizing peace and ancestral blessings, woven with care.

- **Natural Parchment**: To inscribe sigils, connecting the ritual to earth's essence.

- **Charcoal Disk**: A fiery bed to transform the sage and cedar into whispering smoke.

- **Ink and Quill**: Crafted from natural materials, to draw sigils charged with intent.

- **Feather or Fan**: An extension of the spirit's breath, guiding the smoke in sacred dance.

- **Stone or Clay Bowl**: Grounded and sturdy, cradling the burning herbs safely.

   Preparation: Greet the morning's first light in solitude and silence, preparing your sacred space amidst nature's embrace or within your sanctuary. Invite clarity and calm, readying your heart and mind for the ritual.

Crafting the Smudge Bundle:

- **Foundation of Purity**: Position the sage centrally, dedicating it to cleanse and purify.

- **Circle of Strength**: Surround with cedar, its resilience forming a protective embrace.

- **Weave of Harmony**: Bind with sweetgrass, uniting the elements in peaceful accord.

- **Tie of Intent**: Bind the herbs with twine, each wrap sealing intentions within.

- **Knot of Completion**: Finish at the bundle's peak, securing your focused will.

The Ritual:

- **Spark of Creation**: Ignite the sage and cedar upon the charcoal, watching as flames give way to embers and smoke.

- **Sacred Sigils**: On parchment, inscribe your sigils with ink and quill. Focus on your desires, whether for protection, wisdom, or guidance.

- **Smoke Infusion**: Pass each sigil through the sage and cedar smoke, allowing the symbols to absorb the cleansing energy. Visualize the smoke binding with each line, empowering the sigil.

- **Blessing of Thresholds**: At your dwelling's entrance, use the feather to spread smoke, affirming, "With sage, cedar, and sweetgrass, this portal is consecrated, open to light, shielded from shadow."

- **Sanctuary's Heart**: In your home's core, where energies converge, smudge thoroughly. Here, declare, "In this hearth, warmth and harmony reign, safeguarded by ancient spirits."

- **Sigil Activation**: Position your charged sigils in significant spots or carry them as talismans. As the smoke touches each, envision your intentions manifesting, solid and true.

- **Gratitude and Release**: Concluding, weave sweetgrass smoke through your realm, inviting benevolence and joy. Offer thanks to the natural elements, the Appalachian spirits, and the unseen forces at work.

Closing the Ritual: Feel the transformation within and around, a harmonious blend of sigil magic and smoke's purifying dance. Share gratitude for the wisdom of the mountains, the sage, cedar, and sweetgrass. Safely extinguish the smudge, holding its essence for times to come.

This Appalachian Sigil and Smoke Empowerment Ritual stands as a testament to the synergy of earth's gifts and human will, a sacred dance of symbols and scents that empowers, protects, and transforms.

Crafting Specialized Incense Blends for Divination and Dream Work

In the realm of Appalachian magic, where the ancient mountains whisper secrets to those who listen, specialized incense blends serve as vital tools for divination and dream work. These sacred concoctions, steeped in folklore and tradition, are crafted to enhance psychic abilities, facilitate communication with the unseen, and traverse the mystical landscapes of dreams.

Divination Blends

The art of divination, a revered practice within Appalachian mysticism, relies heavily on the clarity and intuition of the practitioner. Incense blends designed for this purpose often contain herbs and resins known to open the third eye and sharpen psychic senses.

Mystic's Vision Blend:

- **Mugwort** (Artemisia vulgaris): A potent ally in divination, mugwort is believed to stimulate psychic visions and enhance prophetic dreams. Its smoke serves as a conduit for spiritual communication.

- **Frankincense Resin** (Boswellia spp.): Revered for its purifying qualities, frankincense elevates the mind, allowing for a deeper connection with the spiritual realm during divination practices.

- **Bay Leaves** (Laurus nobilis): Used for their ability to promote wisdom and enhance intuition. Writing a question on a bay leaf and then burning it in the blend can be a powerful method of receiving guidance.

- **Lavender** (Lavandula spp.): Added for its calming properties, lavender ensures that the divinatory journey remains serene and grounded.

To prepare the Mystic's Vision Blend, mix equal parts of dried mugwort, frankincense resin, crumbled bay leaves, and lavender. Burn this blend during tarot readings, scrying sessions, or pendulum work to open the pathways of intuition and receive clear insights.

Dream Work Blends

The landscape of dreams offers a vast territory for exploration, healing, and communication with the deeper self and the spirit world. Incense blends crafted for dream work incorporate herbs that promote relaxation, induce visionary dreams, and aid in dream recall.

Dream Weaver's Blend:

- **Lavender** (Lavandula spp.): Known for its soothing properties, lavender facilitates a peaceful transition into sleep, setting the stage for meaningful dream work.

- **Chamomile** (Matricaria chamomilla): With its gentle calming effect, chamomile prepares the mind and body for a restful night, encouraging healing dreams.

- **Clary Sage** (Salvia sclarea): Esteemed for its ability to evoke vivid dreams and support lucid dreaming, clary sage is a key component in dream work blends.

- **Cedar** (Juniperus virginiana): Added for grounding, cedar ensures that the dreamer remains tethered to the earth, providing protection during nocturnal journeys.

To create the Dream Weaver's Blend, blend dried lavender, chamomile flowers, clary sage, and cedar shavings in equal parts. Burn this incense as part of your bedtime ritual or when setting intentions for dream work, inviting insightful dreams and clear recollection upon waking.

Customization Tips

The personal connection to one's magical practice is paramount, and as such, customization of these incense blends is encouraged. Consider the following when adapting recipes:

- **Personal Associations**: Reflect on your personal connections with certain plants. If a particular herb resonates strongly with you or has appeared in your dreams or divinations, consider incorporating it into your blend.

- **Local Ingredients**: Embrace the magic of your immediate environment by including herbs and resins native to your region. This not only strengthens your bond with the land but also brings a unique potency to your magical work.

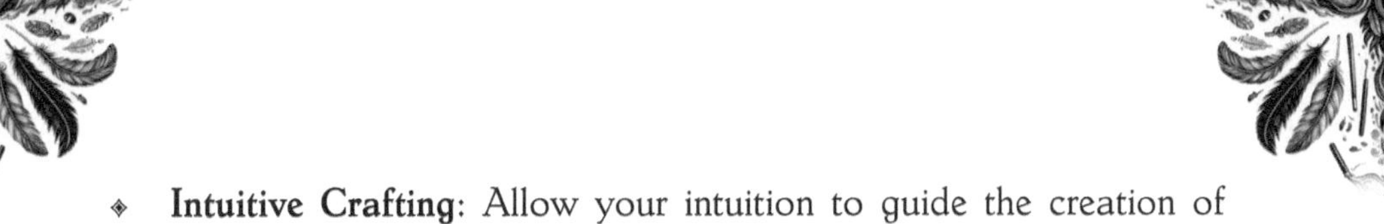

- **Intuitive Crafting**: Allow your intuition to guide the creation of your incense blends. As you mix and match ingredients, focus on your intentions and the specific goals of your divination or dream work. Trust in the wisdom that flows from your hands to your creations.

Through these specialized incense blends, practitioners of Appalachian smoke magic forge a deeper connection with the realms of divination and dreams. Each ingredient, carefully chosen and blended, carries the whispers of ancient knowledge, guiding the seeker on their mystical journey.

MYSTIC'S VISION SMUDGING RITUAL

As the first light of dawn begins to dispel the shadows of the Appalachian night, a profound ritual of insight and vision takes form. The Mystic's Vision Smudging Ritual, inspired by the ancient wisdom of the mountains, is designed to open the gates of perception and connect the practitioner to the deeper currents of intuition and foresight. This ritual harnesses the power of the Mystic's Vision Blend, an incense crafted from sacred herbs and resins known for their divinatory properties.

Materials Needed:

- **Mystic's Vision Incense Blend**: A finely ground mixture of mugwort, frankincense resin, bay leaves, and lavender.

- **Charcoal Disc**: To burn the Mystic's Vision Incense Blend.

- **Fireproof Incense Burner**: To safely hold the charcoal and incense.

- **Candles**: Preferably in colors associated with intuition and psychic vision, such as purple or indigo.

- **Quartz Crystal**: To amplify the energies and intentions of the ritual.

- **Feather or Fan**: For directing the sacred smoke.

- **Journal and Pen**: To record insights and visions that may arise during the ritual.

Preparation: In the stillness of dawn, prepare your sacred space by opening windows to invite in the fresh, crisp air of the mountains, symbolizing a clear and open mind. Arrange your materials on a clean

altar or table, placing the candles in the center with the incense burner nearby.

Crafting the Mystic's Vision Incense:

1. **Blending**: In a small bowl, blend equal parts of the mugwort, frankincense, crumbled bay leaves, and lavender to create the Mystic's Vision Incense Blend.

2. **Charcoal Preparation**: Light the charcoal disc and place it in the fireproof incense burner, waiting until it becomes fully ignited and a layer of gray ash forms.

3. **Incense Offering**: Carefully sprinkle a small amount of the Mystic's Vision Blend onto the hot charcoal, allowing the sacred smoke to rise and fill the air.

The Ritual:

1. **Ignition of Intent**: Begin by lighting the candles, focusing on the flame as a symbol of inner light and clarity. Hold the quartz crystal in your hands, infusing it with your intention to open the channels of psychic vision and intuition.

2. **Cleansing Circle**: Using the feather or fan, gently waft the smoke from the incense blend around your body, starting from the feet and moving upwards in a spiral motion to the crown of your head. Visualize the smoke clearing away any blockages or static within your aura, creating a clear conduit for spiritual insight.

3. **Sacred Space Activation**: Move to each corner of your space, directing the smoke towards the walls, ceiling, and floor, encircling yourself in a protective boundary of aromatic smoke. With each pass, recite a personal mantra or prayer that resonates with your intention for the ritual.

4. **Meditative Insight**: Sit comfortably within your cleansed space, allowing the flickering candlelight and the drifting incense smoke to guide you into a meditative state. Hold the quartz crystal as a focal point for your intentions. Open yourself to any messages, visions, or sensations that may emerge, trusting in the wisdom conveyed by the smoke.

5. **Journaling Reflections**: After your meditation, take some time to journal any insights or visions you experienced. The act of writing

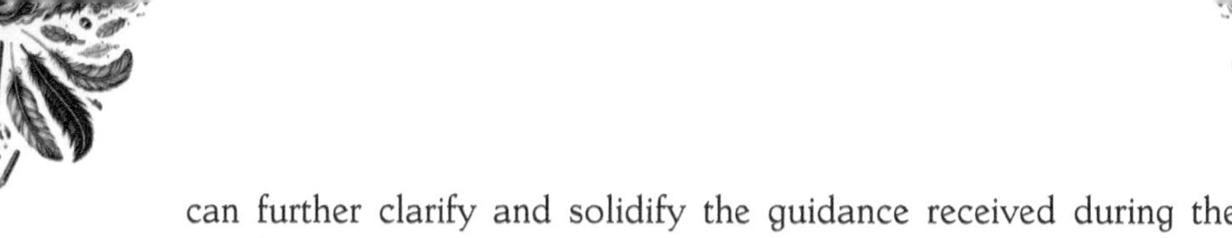

can further clarify and solidify the guidance received during the ritual.

Closing the Ritual: As the incense burns down and the ritual comes to a close, express your gratitude to the elements, the spirits of the herbs, and the guiding forces that have been present. Carefully extinguish the candles and safely dispose of the charcoal. Keep the journal of your insights in a sacred place, returning to it when seeking guidance or reflection.

The Mystic's Vision Smudging Ritual, deeply rooted in the rich soil of Appalachian tradition, serves as a powerful tool for enhancing intuition and forging a deeper connection with the spiritual realm. Through the deliberate blending and burning of sacred herbs, combined with the luminous energy of candlelight and the resonant power of personal intention, this ritual stands as a testament to the enduring magic of smoke and its ability to open the doorways of perception and insight.

Dream Weaver's Ritual

As twilight descends upon the Appalachian wilderness, cloaking the land in a blanket of stars and soft moonlight, the Dream Weaver's Ritual comes to life. This sacred practice is designed to harness the ethereal energies of the night, weaving together the mystical properties of the Dream Weaver's Blend to facilitate profound dream work and spiritual exploration.

Materials Needed:

- **Dream Weaver's Incense Blend**: A finely ground mixture of lavender, chamomile, clary sage, and a hint of mugwort.

- **Charcoal Disc**: For burning the Dream Weaver's Incense Blend.

- **Fireproof Incense Burner**: To hold the charcoal and incense safely.

- **Blue or Silver Candles**: Colors associated with dreams, intuition, and the lunar energies.

- **Moonstone or Amethyst Crystals**: To enhance psychic abilities and promote peaceful sleep.

- **Feather or Fan**: To distribute the sacred smoke with intention.

- **Dream Journal and Pen**: To record insights, visions, or symbols received in dreams.

Preparation: In the serene stillness that only night can bring, prepare your sacred space by dimming the lights and inviting the calm, cooling energies of the evening. Arrange your materials thoughtfully on an altar or table, placing the candles in a way that they cast a soft, comforting glow.

Crafting the Dream Weaver's Incense:

1. **Blending**: Combine the lavender, chamomile, clary sage, and mugwort in a bowl, creating the Dream Weaver's Incense Blend with intentions of tranquility and insight.

2. **Charcoal Preparation**: Ignite the charcoal disc and place it in your incense burner, allowing it to heat until a thin layer of ash forms on its surface.

3. **Incense Offering**: Gently sprinkle a portion of the Dream Weaver's Blend onto the glowing charcoal, welcoming the soothing, aromatic smoke to fill the space.

The Ritual:

1. **Candle Lighting**: Begin by lighting the blue or silver candles, focusing on their flames as beacons of inner wisdom and gateways to the dream realm.

2. **Crystal Charging**: Position the moonstone or amethyst near the incense burner. As the incense burns, envision the crystals absorbing the smoke's properties, becoming potent allies in your dream work.

3. **Smoke Envelopment**: Using the feather or fan, guide the Dream Weaver's smoke around your body, especially around your head and heart, inviting the herbs' essence to permeate your aura and prepare you for deep, insightful dreaming.

4. **Sacred Space**: Move to each corner of your bedroom, allowing the smoke to gently waft through the air, creating a serene, protected space conducive to spiritual dreams and visions.

5. **Intention Setting**: Holding a crystal, close your eyes and set your intentions for your dreams. Whether seeking guidance, healing, or creative inspiration, articulate your desire and visualize it intertwining with the smoke, ascending to the realms of higher consciousness.

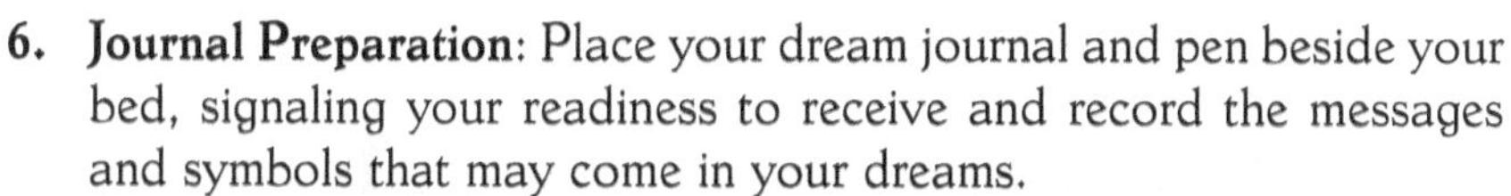

6. **Journal Preparation**: Place your dream journal and pen beside your
    bed, signaling your readiness to receive and record the messages
    and symbols that may come in your dreams.

Closing the Ritual: As the ritual draws to a close, sit quietly for a
few moments, basking in the peace and potential that the night holds.
Offer gratitude to the plants, the crystals, the elements, and the spirits who have aided you. Gently extinguish the candles, ensuring your
space remains a sanctuary of calm. Retire to bed with your mind and
heart open, ready to traverse the dreamscapes with clarity and purpose.

The Dream Weaver's Ritual, steeped in the mystical traditions of Appalachia, serves as a bridge to the subconscious, unlocking the doors
to deeper understanding and spiritual growth. Through the intentional
use of aromatic herbs, the gentle guidance of crystals, and the reflective
glow of candlelight, this ritual embodies a holistic approach to dream
work, inviting the dreamer to explore the vast landscapes of the soul
under the protective canopy of the night sky.

Concluding Thoughts

As we draw the curtains on this enlightening journey through "Sacred Smoke and Mountain Spirits," we reflect on the profound depth and versatility of smoke magic within the rich tapestry of Appalachian traditions. Chapter 10, "Advanced Smoke Magic Techniques," not only serves as a culmination of our exploration but also as a gateway to further discovery and mastery of this ancient art.

Through the integration of incense and smudging with other magical practices such as candle magic and sigils, we've seen how the elemental dance between fire and air can amplify intentions, weaving a more intricate web of protection, insight, and spiritual connection. The crafting of specialized incense blends for divination and dream work opens new pathways for communication with the divine, enhancing our psychic abilities and inviting profound, transformative experiences in the realm of dreams.

This chapter beckons you to push the boundaries of traditional smoke magic, encouraging a creative synthesis of practices that resonate deeply with the spirit of Appalachia. The layered rituals, the incorporation of symbols, and the harmonious blend of scents and elements all serve to elevate your magical work to new heights, fostering a deeper connection with the natural world and the unseen forces that guide and protect us.

As you continue your journey with incense and smudging, let the wisdom of the mountains, the whispers of the forests, and the flow of the rivers inspire your practice. Remember, the true essence of smoke magic lies not just in the herbs you burn or the rituals you perform, but in the intentions you set and the relationships you nurture with the spirits of the land.

May your path be ever guided by the gentle smoke spirals of Appalachian wisdom, and may the sacred fires you kindle illuminate the deepest truths of your soul. Thank you for walking this path with us, for embracing the ancient practices of our ancestors, and for carrying the torch of sacred smoke into the future with reverence and respect.

Chapter 11:
Building Your
Smoke Magic
Practice

Developing a Personal Smoke Magic Practice That Resonates with Appalachian Traditions

Embracing the essence of Appalachian smoke magic is akin to weaving a rich tapestry of tradition, nature, and personal spirituality into the fabric of your daily life. As we delve into the art of developing a personal smoke magic practice, we are reminded of the deep roots that connect us to the Appalachian landscape—a land teeming with ancient wisdom and vibrant energy.

Foundational Principles

The journey into Appalachian smoke magic is a path paved with reverence for the living tapestry of nature. This reverence extends beyond a simple appreciation for nature's beauty; it is an acknowledgment of the vital force that animates every leaf, stone, and stream. To engage with this ancient practice is to enter into a sacred contract with the natural world, one that demands mindfulness, respect, and reciprocity.

Understanding the core principles of this practice requires a deep dive into the ethos of Appalachian traditions, where the land is not merely a backdrop but a central character in the story of life. The mountains, with their ancient wisdom, the forests, teeming with life, and the rivers, coursing with the pulse of the earth, are all integral to the practice of smoke magic. They offer their gifts not as commodities but as sacred offerings, asking in return our attention, respect, and care.

To connect with the land is to understand its rhythms, its cycles, and its needs. It involves listening to the subtle shifts in the air, observing the changes in the foliage, and attuning to the whispers of the wind. This connection is not passive; it's an active engagement that may involve planting native herbs, participating in local conservation efforts, or simply spending time in mindful observation of the natural world.

Customizing Your Practice

Building a smoke magic practice that resonates with your inner being is an intimate process that intertwines the threads of tradition with the unique colors of your personal journey. It's about finding harmony

between the ancient practices of Appalachian magic and the contemporary rhythms of your life.

Diving into the rich lore of Appalachian traditions offers a wellspring of inspiration. The old tales, with their deep connection to the land and its spirits, provide a framework for understanding how smoke magic has been woven into the fabric of life in this region. Yet, the true magic lies in how you take these traditions and make them your own.

Listening to the land and your own spirit might lead you to discover new plants or methods that speak to you. Perhaps the vibrant flame azalea or the resilient rhododendron, both native to the Appalachian region, call to you with their unique energies. Maybe you're drawn to the sound of water, incorporating small bowls of stream water into your rituals to blend the elements of water and air.

The incorporation of personal elements—be it through the choice of herbs, the design of your altar, or the incorporation of music and art that speaks to your soul—is what breathes life into your practice. It transforms it from a series of rituals into a living, breathing extension of your being.

Deepening Your Connection

Exploring Local Flora and Fauna: Beyond the traditional herbs like sage and cedar, the Appalachian region is rich with a diversity of plants, each carrying its own story and energy. Spend time in nature, exploring the hills and valleys, getting to know the local flora. Research their uses, both in traditional medicine and magic, and experiment with incorporating these into your smoke blends. This connection to your immediate environment not only deepens your practice but fosters a profound bond with the land.

Sacred Spaces and Altars: Your sacred space or altar is a physical manifestation of your spiritual journey. Consider the placement of each item: a stone collected from a memorable hike, a feather found on a morning walk, or a piece of coal, a nod to the region's mining heritage. Each object holds energy and intention, creating a tapestry of personal and ancestral stories. As the seasons change, so might your altar, reflecting the ever-evolving journey of your practice.

Integrating Modern Elements: In a world that's ever-evolving, integrating modern elements into your practice can keep it relevant and vibrant. This might mean using digital playlists of Appalachian music or sounds of nature to enhance your rituals, or incorporating modern

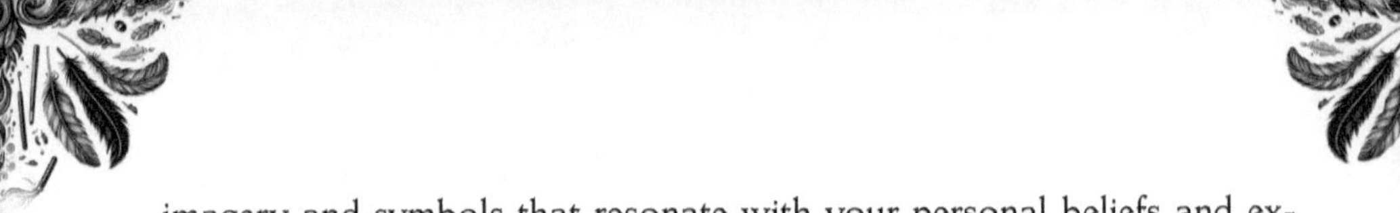

imagery and symbols that resonate with your personal beliefs and experiences. The key is to maintain a balance that honors tradition while embracing the present.

Rituals and Rhythms

Daily Practices: The rhythm of your daily life can be a guiding force in customizing your practice. Morning rituals might include a brief smudging session to welcome the new day, using herbs that invigorate and inspire. Evenings could be reserved for more introspective practices, using calming scents to reflect and wind down. The turning of the seasons can also play a role, with specific rituals and herbs that align with the energies of each season.

Personal and Communal Practices: While much of smoke magic is a deeply personal journey, there's also a communal aspect to consider. Crafting rituals for family gatherings, community celebrations, or even shared moments with friends can add another layer to your practice. These rituals can be adapted to include those who may not share your path but are open to experiencing the warmth and connection it brings.

Reflection and Adaptation: Keeping a journal of your practices, the rituals you perform, the herbs you use, and the experiences you have can be incredibly enriching. It not only serves as a record but as a reflective tool, allowing you to see your growth and adapt your practices as needed. This reflection is a crucial aspect of customization, ensuring your practice remains a true reflection of your journey.

In customizing your smoke magic practice, you weave together the rich tapestry of Appalachian traditions with the unique threads of your personal journey, creating a practice that is deeply rooted in the past yet vibrantly alive in the present. It's a dynamic process, one that evolves with you, offering endless possibilities for growth, learning, and connection.

Integration into Daily Life

Integrating smoke magic into every facet of your daily life transforms mundane moments into sacred rituals, each breath of scented smoke a bridge to the spiritual. This seamless integration begins with the sunrise, greeting the day with smoldering herbs that cleanse and sanctify your personal space, inviting in the freshness of new beginnings. It's a ritual that aligns your spirit with the day's potential, setting a foundation of clarity and peace.

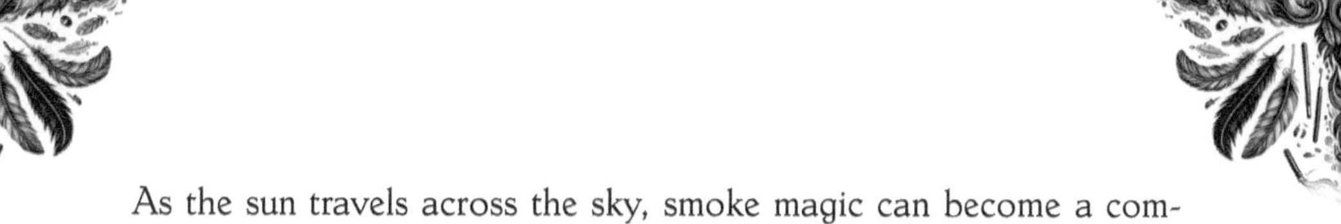

As the sun travels across the sky, smoke magic can become a companion in your daily tasks. A small burner emitting the gentle aroma of sage or pine can sit on your desk, turning work into a consecrated activity, the smoke weaving through your thoughts and intentions, purifying and focusing your mind. In moments of stress or uncertainty, a quick smudging can act like a reset button, dispelling negativity and re-centering your energies.

As dusk falls, the practice shifts to reflection and release. Burning incense with soothing properties, such as lavender or sandalwood, can mark the transition from day to night, signaling to your body and mind that it's time to slow down, to release the day's burdens and embrace the calm of the evening. This ritual can become a sacred pause, a space you carve out for yourself amidst the whirlwind of life, to reflect, to dream, and to simply be.

Incorporating amulets or charm bags into your daily attire can serve as tangible reminders of your protective barriers and intentions. These small talismans, charged with the energies of protective herbs and crystals, act as personal guardians, their presence a constant reminder of your spiritual path and the protective embrace of your practice.

Establishing a dedicated sacred space within your home—a corner, a shelf, or an entire room—offers a physical anchor for your smoke magic practice. This space, adorned with items that hold personal significance, from family heirlooms to found objects from nature, becomes a focal point for deeper rituals or quiet contemplation. It's a physical manifestation of your spiritual journey, evolving with you as you grow and deepen your practice.

As you weave smoke magic into the fabric of your daily life, it becomes more than just a practice; it becomes a way of perceiving the world, a lens through which every moment is infused with magic and meaning. The simple act of lighting incense or passing an object through smoke becomes a profound act of connection to the ancient traditions of the Appalachian lands and to the ever-present spiritual realm.

Remember, the journey into integrating smoke magic into your life is uniquely yours. It's a tapestry woven from your experiences, beliefs, and the whispers of the land and spirits that guide you. Embrace each step, each ritual, as an opportunity to deepen your connection to the magic all around you, crafting a practice that is not only a reflection of the Appalachian traditions but also a profound expression of your own spiritual journey.

Keeping a Magical Journal to Record Recipes, Rituals, and Experiences

In the realm of Appalachian smoke magic, a journal becomes much more than a mere notebook; it is a sacred repository of knowledge, experiences, and personal growth. Keeping a magical journal is akin to creating a map of your spiritual journey, charting the paths you've taken, the landscapes you've traversed, and the horizons yet to be explored.

This journal serves as a tangible connection to your practice, a space where the ethereal meets the material. It is a place to record the whisperings of herbs, the dance of the smoke, and the silent conversations with the spirit realm. By inscribing your experiences, you honor the tradition of oral storytelling inherent in Appalachian culture, giving your own stories a place to reside.

What to Record

Incense Recipes and Herbal Wisdom: Your journal should include detailed recipes of the incense blends you create, noting not just the ingredients but the source of each herb, its significance within Appalachian lore, and the personal meaning it holds for you. Record the sensations, emotions, and memories evoked by each blend, creating a sensory diary of your practice.

Ritual Intentions and Outcomes: Document the rituals you perform, including the phase of the moon, the alignment of the stars, and the season's turn. Describe the intention behind each ritual, the setup of your sacred space, the deities or spirits invoked, and the outcome of the practice. This not only serves as a record but as a guide for future rituals, allowing you to see what resonates most deeply with your spirit.

Personal Insights and Spiritual Encounters: Your journal is also a space for introspection and reflection. Write about the insights gained during your practice, the shifts in your spiritual perceptions, and the encounters with the ancestral spirits or the spirits of the land. These

entries are the heartbeats of your practice, the moments of profound connection and transformation.

Reflection and Growth

Deepening Understanding: Regularly revisiting your journal entries invites a deeper understanding of your practice and its impact on your spiritual journey. It allows you to see patterns emerging, to understand which elements of your practice are most potent and which may need adjustment. This reflective practice is crucial for growth, ensuring that your smoke magic practice remains a living, breathing part of your spiritual path.

Evolving Your Practice: As you reflect on your journal, consider how your practice has evolved and how it might continue to grow. Are there new herbs you feel called to work with? Are there rituals that have become more significant over time? Use your journal as a foundation for experimentation and exploration, pushing the boundaries of your practice while staying rooted in tradition.

Connecting to Ancestral Wisdom: Through your journal, you can forge a deeper connection to the wisdom of those who have walked this path before you. Reflect on the traditional uses of herbs and the ancestral rituals that resonate with your practice. Your journal becomes a bridge between the past and present, allowing you to carry forward the rich heritage of Appalachian smoke magic.

Celebrating the Journey: Above all, your journal is a celebration of your journey within the realm of smoke magic. It is a testament to your commitment to this path, a record of the challenges faced and the victories won. Each entry is a stone laid on the path of your spiritual journey, a reminder of where you've been and a beacon for where you're headed.

In maintaining a magical journal, you're not just keeping a record; you're weaving the tapestry of your practice, stitch by stitch, with each word, each recipe, and each reflection. It's a living document that grows with you, a sacred companion on your journey through the mystical landscapes of Appalachian smoke magic.

CONCLUDING THOUGHTS

As we draw the curtain on this chapter of "Sacred Smoke and Mountain Spirits," we reflect on the journey of intertwining one's spirit with the ancient and venerable traditions of Appalachian smoke magic. Building your practice is not just about mastering techniques or memorizing recipes; it's about forging a deep, personal connection with the land, its spirits, and the smoke that dances between the worlds.

Embracing the foundational principles of respect, connection, and tradition sets the stage for a practice that is not only personal and profound but also reverent and responsible. Customizing your practice allows it to become a true reflection of your spirit, tailored to your path and resonant with the harmonies of the Appalachian landscape.

Integrating smoke magic into the tapestry of your daily life transforms the mundane into the magical, turning each day into an opportunity to engage with the deeper currents of existence. It's in these moments—whether in a simple morning smudging ritual or a nighttime contemplation with incense—that the essence of smoke magic reveals itself, not just as a practice, but as a way of being.

The act of maintaining a magical journal becomes a sacred dialogue between you and the essence of your practice. It's a space where the ephemeral is given weight, where the whispers of the spirits are recorded, and where the growth of your soul is charted. This journal is not just a record; it's a companion on your journey, a mirror reflecting the depth of your experiences and the growth of your spirit.

As you continue to walk the path of smoke magic, let each step be guided by the wisdom of those who have walked before you, by the voices of the herbs and the trees, and by the silent song of the smoke as it rises. Let your practice be a living, breathing homage to the beauty and complexity of the Appalachian traditions, a mosaic of ancient wisdom and personal revelation.

In closing, remember that your practice is a river fed by many streams—tradition, personal intuition, the land, and the community. It is ever-changing, ever-flowing, and ever-deepening. May your journey through the realms of smoke and spirit be filled with discovery, connec-

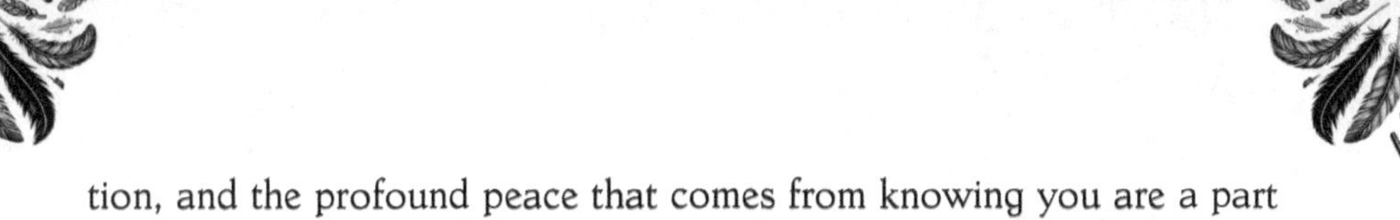

tion, and the profound peace that comes from knowing you are a part of something much larger than yourself—the timeless dance of earth, air, fire, and spirit that is at the heart of Appalachian smoke magic.

Ending Our Journey

Reflecting on the Journey Through the World of Appalachian Smoke Magic

As we draw the curtain on our exploration of "Sacred Smoke and Mountain Spirits: The Art of Appalachian Incense and Smudging," it's a moment to pause and reflect, not just on the knowledge acquired but on the profound journey of personal and spiritual growth we've undertaken together. Delving into the world of Appalachian smoke magic has been more than just an academic or practical endeavor; it has been a voyage into the heart of a living tradition, one that connects us deeply to the earth, its plants, and the spirits that dwell within this ancient landscape.

The Personal Journey

Each page turned and each practice engaged in has been a step along a path that is as much about inner transformation as it is about learning the arts of smudging and incense making. You may have started this journey with curiosity, seeking to understand the mechanics of smoke magic or to add a new dimension to your spiritual practice. Yet, what you've likely found is something far richer: a tapestry of connections to a world that thrums with life and spirit, an invitation to see the natural world, and perhaps even yourself, through a new lens.

The rituals and recipes shared within these pages are more than just methods; they are gateways to experiencing the world in a more enchanted, interconnected way. As you've learned to craft incense blends or to carry out a smudging ritual, you've also been engaging in acts of co-creation with the natural world, learning the language of plants, and tuning into the subtle energies that flow around and through you.

Deepened Connections

With the Plants: Through your engagement with smoke magic, each leaf, each resin, and each wood piece you've worked with has been more than just a material component. They have been teachers, allies, and friends. You've learned to listen to their subtle whispers, understanding their properties not just through texts but through direct, per-

sonal experience. This relationship with the plants is sacred, built on a foundation of mutual respect and gratitude. It asks of you an ongoing commitment to honor their gifts, to approach them with humility, and to partake of their magic in ways that sustain both their well-being and yours.

With the Land: The land of Appalachia, with its rolling hills, dense forests, and clear streams, is not just a backdrop for the practice of smoke magic; it is a living, breathing entity that you've become more attuned to. You've learned to read the signs of the seasons, to feel the pulse of the land beneath your feet, and to recognize the sacredness imbued in every rock, river, and ridge. This deepened connection calls for a continued commitment to protect and preserve the land, to walk upon it lightly, and to contribute to its healing and flourishing.

With the Spirits: The practice of smoke magic has opened doorways to realms beyond the physical, allowing for encounters with the spirits of the land, the ancestors, and the myriad other beings that inhabit the Appalachian spiritual landscape. These relationships, fostered through ritual, respect, and reciprocal exchange, offer profound insights and guidance. They remind us that we are part of a much larger community of beings, seen and unseen, and that our actions in the physical realm reverberate through the spiritual.

Continued Learning and Exploration

Expanding Your Botanical Knowledge: The flora of Appalachia is rich and varied, offering a vast array of plants with magical and medicinal properties. Continue to explore this botanical wealth, seeking to understand not just the uses of these plants but their ecological roles, their life cycles, and the folklore that surrounds them. Engage in field studies, connect with local herbalists, and participate in plant identification workshops to deepen your knowledge and appreciation of Appalachian flora.

Delving Deeper into Lore and Wisdom: The tales, myths, and legends of Appalachia are a treasure trove of wisdom, offering insights into the worldview, values, and spiritual practices of the people who have called these mountains home. Dedicate time to study this rich body of lore, recognizing that each story, each song, and each piece of folklore is a thread in the vibrant tapestry of Appalachian culture. Look for the deeper meanings and spiritual teachings embedded in these tales, and consider how they might inform and enrich your practice of smoke magic.

Fostering Relationships with the Spirits: The spirits of Appalachia, from the guardians of specific places to the ancestral spirits that watch over families and communities, are ever-present companions on the journey of smoke magic. Continue to cultivate these relationships through regular offerings, rituals, and dialogues. Seek to understand the ways in which these spirits communicate and the forms of reciprocity they desire, always approaching them with respect, openness, and a willingness to listen.

Embracing the Journey as Ongoing: Recognize that the path of smoke magic is not linear but cyclical, mirroring the cycles of nature that are so central to Appalachian spirituality. There is always more to learn, more to experience, and deeper levels of connection to be attained. Approach this journey with a spirit of curiosity, wonder, and humility, knowing that each step forward is both a deepening and an expansion of your relationship with the plants, the land, and the spirits.

As you continue to walk this path, let the smoke be your guide, your connector, and your protector, weaving you ever more tightly into the fabric of this magical tradition. Carry with you the lessons of the past, the practices of the present, and the promise of future discoveries, knowing that you are part of a living, breathing tradition that spans generations and speaks to the heart of what it means to live in harmony with the natural and spiritual worlds.

Preservation of Tradition

The practices of smoke magic that have been shared within these pages are more than just personal spiritual tools; they are threads in the larger tapestry of Appalachian tradition. As keepers of this wisdom, it becomes our responsibility to ensure that these practices are not lost to time. Sharing this knowledge with others—whether through teaching, writing, or the simple act of practicing openly—serves as an act of preservation, keeping the tradition alive and vibrant.

This sharing, however, goes beyond mere transmission of knowledge. It's about passing on the reverence for the plants, the respect for the land, and the acknowledgment of the spirits that are integral to smoke magic. By embodying these values in our actions and sharing them with others, we contribute to the continuity and vitality of this tradition. Whether you find yourself in the role of teacher, mentor, or simply a practitioner whose life is a testament to these practices, you become a link in the chain that stretches back into the past and forward into the future.

Adaptation and Evolution

While the preservation of tradition is crucial, it's equally important to recognize that traditions are living things. They grow, change, and evolve, shaped by the hands and hearts of those who practice them. As Appalachian smoke magic continues to be embraced by new practitioners, it will inevitably adapt to meet the needs, perspectives, and contexts of those individuals and communities.

This process of adaptation is not a dilution of the tradition but rather a sign of its vitality. It's an indication that the practices are robust and flexible enough to remain relevant and meaningful in a changing world. As you continue your journey with smoke magic, allow yourself to be an active participant in this evolution. Experiment, innovate, and adapt the practices to suit your path, always with an eye to the core principles and values that underpin the tradition. In doing so, you ensure that Appalachian smoke magic remains a living, breathing tradition that speaks to the hearts of future generations.

Closing Gratitude and Blessing

As we conclude our journey through the mist-shrouded mountains and verdant valleys of Appalachian smoke magic, let us take a moment to offer our deepest gratitude. To the plants that have shared their essence and their spirit with us, we offer our heartfelt thanks. To the land that has nurtured and sustained these practices, we express our enduring reverence. To the spirits that have guided and protected us, we extend our sincere appreciation. And to the ancestors and elders who have passed down this wisdom through the ages, we acknowledge our profound debt.

May this book serve not just as a guide to the practices of smoke magic but as a beacon, calling forth those who feel the stirrings of this ancient tradition in their souls. May it light your way as you walk the path of discovery, connection, and co-creation with the natural and spiritual worlds.

And now, as you step forward from this shared journey into the continuing adventure of your own path, I offer you this blessing:

May the smoke from your fires be a bridge between the worlds, carrying your prayers and intentions to the spirits. May the plants be your allies and teachers, sharing their wisdom and protection with you. May the land hold you in its embrace, guiding your steps and nurturing

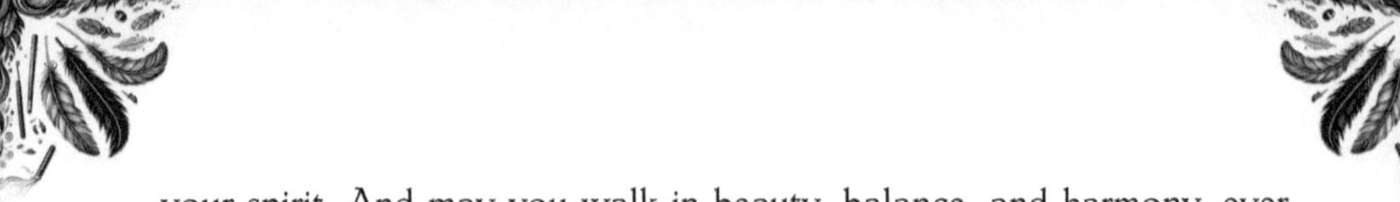

your spirit. And may you walk in beauty, balance, and harmony, ever attuned to the magic that surrounds you and flows through you.

Go forth with the blessings of the mountains and the forests, the rivers and the streams, the spirits and the ancestors. Carry the wisdom of smoke magic in your heart, and let its fragrance be a constant reminder of the sacred web of life to which we all belong.

In closing, remember that the end of this book is not the end of your journey but a new beginning, a gateway to deeper exploration, understanding, and connection. Walk in peace, walk in power, and walk in magic, now and always.

In the gentle embrace of dawn, beneath the watchful gaze of ancient Appalachian peaks, may your path be ever clear. As the smoke rises, weaving through the whispering leaves, so too may your spirit soar, guided by the wisdom of the land and the voices of the ancestors.

Blessed be your hands that gather herbs with reverence; blessed be your heart that beats in rhythm with the earth; blessed be your breath that stirs the embers into flame. May the sacred smoke that curls around your soul carry away all that weighs you down, leaving only peace and purity in its wake.

As you walk this path of smoke and magic, may the spirits of the mountain watch over you. May the winds carry your intentions to the corners of the world, and may the fire ignite your courage. Let the waters soothe your spirit, and the earth ground your being.

In every leaf that rustles, in every flame that dances, may you find a story. In every herb that burns, in every dream that whispers, may you find a lesson. Take these gifts of nature, these blessings of the ancestors, and weave them into your life, a tapestry of magic and mystery.

Go forth with the blessing of the Appalachian winds, the strength of the cedar, the wisdom of the sage, and the peace of the sweetgrass. May your journey through smoke and spirit be deep and rich, filled with the wonder of discovery and the comfort of homecoming.

So mote it be.